For the families of those Christian missionaries who didn't come back, who died, or still linger in prison for the cause of the Gospel. Messengers who were willing to risk it all.

Janie Jacks

THE MACAU MAVERICK

AUSTIN MACAULEY PUBLISHERS™
LONDON * CAMBRIDGE * NEW YORK * SHARJAH

Copyright © **Janie Jacks** 2024

All rights reserved. No part of this publication may be reproduced, distributed, or transmitted in any form or by any means, including photocopying, recording, or other electronic or mechanical methods, without the prior written permission of the publisher, except in the case of brief quotations embodied in critical reviews and certain other non-commercial uses permitted by copyright law. For permission requests, write to the publisher.

Any person who commits any unauthorized act in relation to this publication may be liable to criminal prosecution and civil claims for damages.

All of the events in this memoir are true to the best of author's memory. The views expressed in this memoir are solely those of the author.

Ordering Information
Quantity sales: Special discounts are available on quantity purchases by corporations, associations, and others. For details, contact the publisher at the address below.

Publisher's Cataloging-in-Publication data
Jacks, Janie
The Macau Maverick

ISBN 9798889101185 (Paperback)
ISBN 9798889101192 (Hardback)
ISBN 9798889101208 (ePub e-book)

Library of Congress Control Number: 2023915690

www.austinmacauley.com/us

First Published 2024
Austin Macauley Publishers LLC
40 Wall Street, 33rd Floor, Suite 3302
New York, NY 10005
USA

mail-usa@austinmacauley.com
+1 (646) 5125767

I am especially indebted to my friend, Carolyn Brown, a lifelong English and and Drama instructor who read every word and helped me edit for over three years. She believed the story was important for the world to hear and gladly volunteered her time to the project.

Prologue

The dog was an anomaly of nature. Ugly did not do him justice. A dachshund that lived down the street had proved himself—and the German Shepherd female that lived next door had been an agreeable and willing participant.

The result of their illicit union was a freak. Head of a Shepherd, body of a dachshund—with legs four inches from the ground. Extremely and incredibly awkward. All-in-all, a very ugly dog. His one redeeming characteristic was that he had the heart of a giant.

This faithful and loving creature was the master and owner of a boy whose genealogical background was in total contrast to his dog's suspected parentage. The boy was descended from a strong lineage of men who were fit, athletic, and rugged—culled from those who had endured the hardships of settling Western America—survivors of the fittest who had passed their genes down to the next generation.

Somewhere in the boy's heritage, an Englishman bestowed the proper name of Swan upon the family. The boy carried his name well.

His mother came from a different lineage. College educated. Socially astute. People educated in the fields of math, physics, and engineering. Specialists and teachers. Correct speech and diction. She was impeccable, with an understanding of the advantages that correct posture and proper clothing could give you.

Members of America's greatest generation, the boy's parents emerged from the 1920s Depression determined to raise children worthy of their inheritance. Righteous people who attended a local church each Sunday, making sure that their children were properly trained in the fundamentals of righteousness as well.

No generation ever understands the next. Their expectations are never exactly duplicated and handed down—despite all efforts to do so. But one thing was a constant in the nineteen forties when it came to raising children.

Sons were expected to succeed. Girls were not, and the Swans had produced only one son.

The boy felt no pressure. He didn't know he was supposed to succeed. He was just a kid with a dog—a dog that chased him around the house every day after school. Running fast, tightening a circular path—with the unwieldy dog flailing along trying to keep up and make the tight turns. Eventually, the dog would flop to the ground on his side as his legs continued to gallop and churn the air, his tongue flapping from side to side.

The dog's name was Tango. Tango was pitifully stupid. The boy's name was Bill—and he was very, very smart.

Chapter 1

Every boy falls in love in the eighth grade. Usually, they all fall in love with the same girl—the gorgeous, budding, classic beauty who is completely out of their reach. The one girl in their class who isn't interested in dorks. And all eighth-grade boys are dorks.

Janet Morgan was that ethereal, unattainable girl in the class behind Bill. By ninth grade, she was every mother's dream of a someday-final-chapter for their sons. Thick dark hair. Poise, charm, and impeccable character. The kind of girl who would never need a guy to make her feel that she was special. She simply was special. She didn't have to try.

Whether a boy is stupid or smart, it makes no difference when the girl is pretty. And she was definitely pretty.

"So, did'ja ask her? Did she say she'd go to the movies with you? What did'ja say to her?"

Every guy in Bill's group of friends had put their two cents in, and agreed on the correct opening line that was needed to engage conversation with a female, "Ya' wanna' get lucky?"

The fact that none of them had ever tried that line didn't deter their hopes. It was definitely the wrong line—absolutely wrong. But none of them knew that. None of them had ever gotten close enough to a real girl to use it anyway.

Eighth-grade boys are notoriously stupid. Bumbling, falling over their feet stupid. An adolescent mixture of brains and body parts that are not enough, or are too much. Trying to learn the intricacies of engaging the opposite sex while maintaining their own inflated self-image of "cool." The very concept of accomplishing that task is an oxymoron.

Both Bill and Janet's fathers were Baptist church deacons, and their families sat near each other every Sunday morning, Sunday night, and Wednesday night as well. Church life rotated around a never-ending circle of

Sunday sermons, socials, youth camps, outings and parties which—even though she was a year younger—put the two in a parallel world of contact.

It turned out that he didn't need a line to gain her attention after all. He reached across the pew for her hand one night, and she didn't move it away. His heart fluttered.

Junior high allows no opportunities for young people to be alone. They had to be content with holding hands at church, or an occasional dance at a heavily sponsored teen-town weekend event.

All through his ninth-grade year, Bill watched as the older boys, Juniors, and Seniors with cars, snapped up the eligible girls in the Sophomore and Freshman classes, sweeping them out of reach of guys who had no wheels. All he could do was hope that she didn't succumb to a boyfriend with a car.

His long-awaited male rite of passage came at the end of his sophomore year. A driver's license. License in hand, he immediately called, "Janet, would you like to go to a movie with me?"

By God's grace, she said, "Yes." He was ecstatic.

"Hey, guys," Bill told his friends. "I got a date with Janet."

They began pumping him up for the big night, "Just move yer' arm around the back of the seat when they turn the lights down. Kinda slow."

They gave him other instructions as well—instructions that he knew were out of the question.

He didn't tell them he was too shy to even try to kiss her good night. Which turned out to be the last chance he would get for six more years—because, after that one date, he messed up any opportunity for another. Big time.

Two weeks after taking her to the movie, she asked him to go on a hayride with her. "It's the annual Sadie-Hawkins-Day girl-ask-boy event," she explained. "I don't have my driver's license yet, so my dad will bring me over to your house to pick you up."

When she knocked at the door, Mr. Swan opened the screen to let her in. "Are you here to see Bill?" he asked.

"Yes. He's going to the hayride with me."

After an uncomfortable period of silence, Mr. Swan stuttered, "Well." Not knowing quite what to say next. He could see Janet's father waiting for her in the car, and would gladly have wrung his son's neck at that moment.

"I'm really sorry, Janet, but he's not here," he told her. "He went to the movie with his friends. Maybe he got the day wrong. I don't see how he could have forgotten."

There are many things a woman can bear. Rejection, abuse, criticism, insults, and anger. But to be forgotten is unforgivable. It is the unpardonable sin, and this girl was definitely not forgettable. She could have asked any guy in the entire high school to go to the Sadie-Hawkin's-Day hayride with her and they would have tripped over themselves at the chance.

At 11 o'clock that night, Bill arrived home, oblivious about the forgotten date until his father met him at the front door. "What were you thinking!" Mr. Swan yelled at his son. "That poor girl was mortified, and if I was her, I would never speak to you again. You absolutely will explain this to her dad; you will apologize for our entire family. This is inexcusable. Give me your keys. You're grounded until further notice."

Bill's face had gone from happy-go-lucky to devastated in a heartbeat. He had never heard so many words all at once from his father before—who was totally furious and completely disgusted with his son. He was furious and disgusted with himself as well.

"You will apologize. Do it before tomorrow is over—to her, and to her parents as well. And I hope they are understanding. They're raising three girls. I doubt they have any idea how stupid boys can be."

Chapter 2
High School

A few weeks later, he asked her to go to the movies again. She didn't hesitate to say no.

"No," she said as she walked away.

He never had the nerve to ask again. He was dead in the water. Only an idiot would forget he had a date with her. And he was obviously an idiot.

More than ever, he wanted to impress her; when a boy has been soundly rejected, he has something to prove. To himself—if to nobody else.

Football hero, best all-around athlete, mayor for a day, class president, valedictorian, president of the student council, congressional page, an appointment to the Naval academy—you name it, he did it all before he graduated. An overachiever on academic steroids. What was there not to like?

She wasn't buying it. But when there was an event, when students gathered, there were electrical connections between them without a wire. A crackling undercurrent that wouldn't go away. Both of them circling and moving away from the obvious elephant who was also in the room.

It's impossible to forget your first love.

Chapter 3
The Guitar

The guitar was in the front window of Sandusky's seed and supply. Not the usual place to feature a musical instrument in the window, but Sandusky's also served as the local gathering place for every old-timer, red-neck, and wanna-be in that part of Oklahoma. If you wanted to learn how to play the guitar, Sandusky's was where you went to sit, watch, listen, and give it a try. Especially on Saturday mornings.

"I need a dozen of them Jet-star tomato plants and a cuppl'a bags of mulch. Would'ja sack it up fer me and I'll pick 'em up on the way out," a customer asked.

Mr. Sandusky sold guitars along with seeds and farm supplies. All the come-to-town-on-Saturday yahoos would stop in to buy their plant and garden needs, then stay and listen to the pickers and strummers.

One wall of the plant and seed store held cucumber plants, onions, potatoes, seedlings, and such. The other wall was lined with the latest pick-and-fiddle supplies along with guitars, all the way from cheap to the totally out-of-reach.

There was always someone in bib-overalls doing a jig to the music, their feet tapping the wooden floors to the sound of someone picking and strumming on a banjo. Or singing an off-key somebody-done-somebody-wrong song that appealed to the brokenhearted. Bill was hooked. He definitely had a broken heart. He bought a guitar like the one in the window on credit.

Fifteen dollars a month for ten months—earned with after-school jobs mowing lawns. A '59 C.F. Martin triple-zero-eighteen, for one hundred and fifty dollars. It didn't take him long to get the hang of the thing; he learned every chord in every key.

"No self-respecting Oklahoma guitarist uses a capo to fret the strings," he informed the pick-and-grinners at the feed store—which earned him a round of applause. As well as respect.

If you didn't have an instrument, a comb wrapped with wax paper would let you hum along with the group. Sandusky kept a roll of wax paper on the counter for anyone who wanted to join in, since every "Brill-cream, a little dabb'll do ya" guy in Oklahoma had a comb in his pocket to keep his hair in line.

Chapter 4
College Slump

High-school graduation came and went, followed by a huge let-down. When you've been the big duck in a little puddle—as he had been in his small Oklahoma hometown—going to college was an enormous transition.

He had all the academic qualifications and personal credentials to be there, but Oklahoma University was big, he was anonymous, and no longer accountable to anybody. Like almost every other boy from a small town who transferred to a huge school, he floundered.

It wasn't that the curriculum was difficult—he had never made a B in his life. The problem was that he didn't have to study, and as a result, had too much free time on his hands. He also had no background or training in how-to-make-a-friend. He had always been the guy in high school that everyone wanted to be 'around'—the guy everybody wanted to run with. But at college, no one knew or gave a flip who he had been back home. He had become an instantaneous nobody.

The outcome was predictable. Every college freshman faces the same dilemma—the search to figure out who they are. Where do they fit in? Who do they run with?

Some figure it out, but some take a shortcut and gain automatic so-called-friends. They join a frat. Which is what he did; it was a very bad choice.

By the time the year was over, he was disgusted with his frat lifestyle and disappointed in himself. Righteousness had made a left turn, and he didn't know how to fix it. How does a guy fix stupid anyway? He had never before in his life failed at anything he set his mind to. It was a new experience that he wished he hadn't experienced.

Academically, his grades were exceptionally good.
He wasn't.

Chapter 5
Floating the Arkansas

"Hey!" Bill whacked his best friend Johnny on the back. "Good to see you, bud. How was Brazil?"

"Disaster. How was OU?"

Johnny was home from his senior year in Brazil as a foreign exchange student.

"Not great," Bill said. "I didn't adjust very well. Didn't make any real friends. I joined a frat, didn't walk the straight and narrow, and don't like how that went. I plan to spend the summer getting myself back to who I really am, and prepare to face it all over again in the fall. How about you? What made Brazil a disaster? Did you graduate?"

"Yeah. I graduated. But the family I was assigned to live with—they didn't expect the exchange program to be so expensive. Nobody's gonna believe this but it's the truth—they tried to get rid of me in order to get out of their contract. They tried to knock me off."

"You're nuts!" Bill exclaimed.

"I said you wouldn't believe it. I spent two months in intensive care bleeding internally, till the doctors found out my stomach was full of ground glass. The exchange family laced the food I ate and it tore up my gut; I almost kicked the bucket."

"Good grief, Johnny. Obviously, you survived; how are you now?"

"I'm OK. The doctor said it was a miracle it didn't finish me off; however, there was an upside. The Brazilian president took me home to live with his family and hired a private doctor to take care of me for the rest of the academic year. I had a private room, fantastic food, swimming pool. The works. He was concerned the incident would cause international repercussions between the United States government and the Brazilian student exchange program."

"What happened to the host family? Did they get locked up?"

"I never heard or saw anything about it in the newspapers. The doctors knew what was wrong with me, but there wasn't any way to prove who did it. It wouldn't have helped the condition I was in. I survived. That's what counted."

That weekend, their old high school crowd reserved the city pool for an evening of get-together. Johnny hit a home run entertaining everyone with the story of his life in the home of Brazil's top dog. He had always been good at telling stories, and the fact that this story was true—if slightly exaggerated—made the evening with friends memorable and a lot of fun.

Janet was there. Bill spoke; she nodded, then ignored him. Trying to gain her attention looked hopeless.

"She's not even gonna give you a smile," Johnny told him. "Four years later and you're getting nowhere. You might as well give it up!"

"Not yet," Bill said. "Not yet."

The two boys were facing an entire summer with nothing, in particular, to do—which is never a good thing.

"Since I'm getting nowhere with women," Bill said, "I'll tell you what we otta' do. Let's float the Arkansas; government's gonna block it off with locks and dams, and after they block it, nobody will ever be able to float it again. We could make it to New Orleans before the summer's over."

That evening, Bill shared his plan with his mom and dad.

"Johnny and I are gonna float down the Arkansas to New Orleans before they close the river and build the dam at Dardanelle. Johnny's dad has a fourteen-foot Jonboat with a ten-horsepower motor we can use."

"No! Absolutely not!" his mother exclaimed. "What are you thinking! Do you have any idea how foolish that is? How dangerous that would be! You could be killed."

Bill waited on his father to also say no. The last time his dad had chastised him was when Bill had forgotten his date with Janet—so he was expecting a negative response. There was a moment of silence, then shock, when his father said, "Marge, he's going to go."

His mother was so unprepared for the pronouncement of his father's authority as head of the household, that she took one step backward, stuttered, and said, "OK. If you think it's alright."

Bill had never heard his dad buck his mother's opinion before; he was as startled at his father's support as his mother was.

He immediately went to his room and began packing his gear before either of them reconsidered.

Chapter 6
The Arkansas

The upper Arkansas was nothing but shallow water and sand in 1963. In the early days of the westward American movement, many a family trying to cross the river had lost a wagon, along with a team of horses or pair of oxen to the treacherous Arkansas River's quicksand. It sucked you in. It sucked you down.

Watching a desperate animal sink, straining to keep its nose above a quagmire that it couldn't possibly escape, broke many a hopeful westward dreamer's heart. Having to helplessly watch as the animal took its final breath and gave up its life to the relentless unforgiving Arkansas River quicksand—taking the wagon and everything that was on it down to a slow and agonizing death. It ended the western dream for many families who couldn't go back and couldn't go forward without their wagons, horses, or supplies.

Johnny's father backed the boat trailer down a rutted dirt road into the water just north of Muskogee. The two boys threw their gear into the boat, then tugged it off the trailer into the Arkansas River, trying to find a current to move them—so they could clear the shallow river bottom and start the motor.

"We'll call you to come to get us when we get to New Orleans," Johnny yelled over his shoulder to his father.

"If we get there," Bill muttered under his breath as they pushed off the treacherous sandbars with their paddles to get to deeper water, looking for a channel to keep from getting stuck.

"Where's the channel?" Johnny asked.

"Can't tell," Bill replied. "This may be harder than we thought. Stick a paddle down and push or we're gonna be hung up in mud before we ever get started."

With no way to determine where the channel was, they were at the mercy of the murky water, sand, and mud of the treacherous Arkansas River.

Over and over again their propeller hit a sandbar, shearing off the cotter pin from the force of the impact. Without the cotter pin attached to the shaft, the motor was dead in the water; and without the motor, they were stuck in the middle of nowhere. Up a creek with nothing but paddles.

"Lift that shaft," Bill yelled. "I'll hold the boat steady until you get the cotter pin changed."

Johnny jumped off the back of the boat, lifted the shaft and propeller, and fixed the connection as Bill watched. Bill needed to learn how to change pins and take his turn in the water. They had brought over thirty spare cotter pins with them when they left Muskogee, but replacing one meant someone had to get out of the boat—which was a dangerous problem.

"I'm sinking," Johnny screamed. "Pull the boat forward," he yelled. "Pull me out of this!"

He had lifted the stuck propeller up and out of the sand bar, only to get stuck in quicksand himself. He was up to his shins in the sucking sand, unable to free himself with nothing to hold onto but the back of the boat.

Without a motor, the only way out was to pull. Bill hopped out of the front of the boat into the murky water, got his footing on the river bottom, and began to pull with every ounce of strength he could muster, praying that he didn't end up stuck in quicksand as well. He could hear the terrible sucking sound of the quicksand as he strained to pull the boat forward and help Johnny free his legs.

Sweat was streaming down both of their faces when Johnny finally pulled loose and hauled himself back into the boat. They jabbed their oars into the water, pushing off the sandbank, desperately searching for deeper water—trying to find the channel so they could start the motor and begin moving again.

Before the day was over, they had been stuck three times and lost three cotter pins. At the rate they were going, they would run out of pins before the Arkansas River ever reached the Mississippi.

Unexpected adversity produced exhaustion, which completely overtook them by the end of the first day. They moored the boat on the bank, ate cold pork and beans out of a can, unfolded their army issue cots, covered themselves with mesh mosquito netting, and fell into a dead sleep.

"Wake up!" Bill screamed. It was pitch dark in the middle of the night. "Help me with this boat!" Bill was knee-deep in water holding onto the boat trying to drag it higher up the bank. "Help me! This thing has torn loose; it's floating off and we're going to lose it."

Bill had been jarred awake soaking wet. Ocean tides traveling up the Mississippi River from the Gulf of Mexico had raised the level of the Arkansas, and the boys had set up their cots too close to the banks.

Johnny fell off his cot into the rising water. "What! What's happening?" Johnny yelled.

"I'm over here," Bill yelled. "Grab that rope and pull with me or we're gonna lose our boat!"

It was so dark Johnny couldn't figure out where he was much less where Bill was. He dragged his cot out of the water, repositioning it further up the bank as his eyes adjusted to the night and he could see the boat. He pulled, losing his footing in the mud, slipping and sliding with every step, helping Bill get the boat back on land and tied to a tree.

Naked and shivering, they spread their clothes on bushes to dry, crawled back into their wet cots, pulled dripping mosquito netting over their bodies, and instantly fell into a dead sleep.

"One more lesson learned the hard way," Bill told Johnny the next morning. "We've got to spend nights further from the water's edge, nearer the woods."

"If we're gonna' be sleeping further from the water and closer to the woods at night, maybe we should think about coyotes? Bobcats? What's out there anyway?"

"Which do you want? Coyotes, or snakes. We've already seen moccasins in the water, and they're unpredictable; they'll come straight at you. A coyote howls, so you know it's coming. I don't want to end up dead after a cotton mouth bites me. Let's camp further off the banks into the woods and take our chance with the coyotes and bobcats."

Between the treacherous river and rising tides on the banks, their adventure was turning into a nightmare. And it had just begun.

Chapter 7
Dardanelle Dam

In 1963, the dam at Dardanelle was barely past the stage of being a dream for United States Senator Robert S. Kerr—a series of water projects and dams that would make the Arkansas River into a navigable inland waterway system by increasing the depth of the shallow Arkansas River. The government named it the McClellan-Kerr-Arkansas-River-Navigation-System.

The final project would result in a series of locks and dams—eventually creating an inland port ending near Tulsa at Catoosa, Oklahoma. A port! Opening midwestern Oklahoma all the way to the Gulf of Mexico and the Atlantic Ocean beyond. An economic windfall for the landlocked state.

Born in a log cabin in Indian Territory, Kerr was a staunch, tee-totaling Sothern Baptist man with a vision for the economic future of his home state. Growing up, and later as the state's governor, Kerr had seen the devastation caused by flooding on the Arkansas and its tributaries. Devastation occurred numerous times every year as a result of the river's shallow bed and propensity to overflow its banks, destroying everything in its path.

The shallowness of the Arkansas also prevented any river traffic from ever reaching Oklahoma. Oil, wheat, livestock, and other products that the state was known for had to be distributed to the rest of the world by much more expensive modes of transportation. The series of locks and dams would be Kerr's legacy for the state.

Dardanelle was the first dam project to be built—and preliminary construction was underway. Bill and Johnny's plan was to beat the Dardanelle's completion—to be able to brag and say that they had driven a Jonboat all the way from northeast Oklahoma down the Arkansas to the Mississippi—and on to the Gulf. But actually doing it had become a huge challenge.

Days passed, more cotter pins were torn up by sandbars, and both young men had repeatedly been stuck in quicksand by the time they reached the Dardanelle construction.

"Look at that," Johnny exclaimed.

"What?" Bill asked.

"There's a bunch of people standing around on the banks—next to where they're working on the dam."

"That's strange. What'a ya think they're doing?"

"I don't know, but they're looking at us."

Their arrival was greeted by a large crowd. Word had spread about the boy's Huckleberry Finn adventure, and not only were hundreds of people gathered on the banks to surprise them, the Associated Press had picked up the news and was waiting by the river for them to arrive as well. The press wanted an interview and some film of the boy's adventure for the nightly news. Unbeknownst to Bill and Johnny, they had become a national phenomenon.

Questions were fast and furious. "What prompted you to do this?" someone yelled. "Why are you two floating down the Arkansas," followed by, "Why are you trying to do it in a Jonboat? Isn't that dangerous; did you get stuck; what all did you bring on board with you; did you encounter any quicksand?"

Bill and Johnny weren't interested in answering the crowd or the Associated Press questions. They were exhausted; all they wanted to do was get back in the water on the other side of the construction mess, and keep moving. They were totally unprepared for the onslaught.

There they were, stranded, sitting in their boat, needing help to navigate around the construction. They were dirty, pitiful, and unnerved by the number of people watching them from the river banks—not really knowing what to do next. The dam hadn't been finished and the river was full of girders and other construction materials that blocked them from proceeding.

"What do you think we should do?" Bill asked Johnny.

"Well, it's a sure thing we can't just sit here in the water and pray for God to send a crane to lift us up over this mess."

Bill scanned the crowd and locked eyes with a friendly face in the mob, an old man leaning on a tree—off to the side of the rest of the people. Bill yelled at the man over the loud unending reporter's questions, "Sir! Do you know anybody with a hitch who can pull us out of the water and get our boat to the other side of this construction?"

"Yep. You betcha'. Gim'me a bit," the old timer replied. He wandered off out of sight, then came back a few minutes later accompanied by a fellow driving a flatbed truck loaded with granite tombstones.

"I'll be glad to hep'ya," the truck driver offered. "Can ya'all pull yer' boat up onto the shore? If you can get'er up out of the water, me and some'a these fella's standing around'll give you a hand loadin' it onto my truck. We'll git'cha back in the water a few feet on down a-ways'. River water ain't been blocked up anywhere yet. We'll have you floating agin' in no time a'tall."

Some of the others that were standing around watching what was going on offered to help load the boat onto the truck. The old man and the truck driver shoved the crowd out of the way and gave Bill and Johnny room to drag the boat ashore.

With the help of the old-timers and volunteers, the boys loaded their boat onto the flatbed truck behind the tombstones—relieved to escape the questions of the reporters who continued to hound them. They didn't have an answer as to why they were doing what they were doing anyway. They just wanted to get on with it.

Once the boat was secured, Bill and Johnny hopped on the back end behind the tombstones and their boat, and the truck owner drove them to the other side of the construction. When they were clear of all the people, the boys dragged their Jonboat off the truck and pushed it down the bank, back into the waters of the Arkansas River.

"Thanks for helping us out," they said to the truck driver.

They yelled goodbye to the old men, then set out to finish their trip down the Arkansas River to the Mississippi delta. Relieved to have escaped the broo-hah-hah of the crowd that had gathered on the river banks to greet them.

Chapter 8
Twenty-Gauge Shotgun

"We have to stop somewhere soon," Bill informed Johnny. "We're almost out of drinking water and gasoline."

Bill steered the boat underneath the four-lane bridge on Interstate 440, the highway into Little Rock—then secured the boat out of sight of the road. He didn't want any more experiences with crowds of people.

"What else do we need?" Johnny asked him.

"Canned stuff. Beans, any kind of meat in a can. Tuna, chicken, chili, tamales. Whatever you can find. You get the stuff; I'll stay with the boat so somebody doesn't steal it."

Johnny opened the Folgers coffee can that held their money and asked, "You think twenty will be enough?"

"Better take twenty-five and be sure," Bill answered.

Johnny stepped out of the boat, crawled up the muddy bank to the road and thumbed a ride into town, leaving Bill behind to guard the boat.

Three hours later, loaded down with brown paper bags, Johnny hitched a ride back to the bridge with a man who was hauling lumber. "Thanks for the help," he told the trucker.

"Not so fast." The driver stepped out of the truck and slammed the door. "I need some money for heppin' ya."

"You gotta be kidding, I'm not giving you any money," Johnny told him. "I hitched. You picked me up. I don't have any money anyway." Johnny began to slide down the bank of the Arkansas with his hands and arms full of sacks, yelling, "Bill! Help! Give me a hand with these bags."

The truck driver stormed around the front of the truck hollering, "I want sum' money for my trouble. Ya needs to pay me for driving you here and hauling yer sacks."

Bill reached for the loaded twenty-gauge shotgun at the bottom of the boat and yelled at the man, "He hitched. You picked him up. You aren't driving a cab and we're not giving you any money. You better get back in your truck, mister, or I'm going to shoot you."

The rough, scruffy-looking man was heading toward the boat, but when Bill pointed the gun at him, he considered the unfavorable options and decided to retreat. Swearing and cursing, he got back into his truck and drove away, flashing the finger as he left.

"Hand me some of those sacks," Bill yelled at Johnny. "Before he comes back."

He loaded the supplies onto the boat as fast as possible, as Johnny scrambled back up the embankment to collect things that had fallen during his escape—keeping an eye on the road in case the angry man returned. He handed Bill what he had collected and hopped into the boat as Bill pushed off the bank and moved back into the channel to start the motor.

Out of sight of the bridge, Johnny caught his breath and asked, "Would'ja really have shot him?"

"I don't know," Bill replied. "But if he had taken one step closer, I guess I would've found out."

"Thanks for the cover," Johnny told him. "When you pointed that thing at him, I was scrambling to get out of the way to make sure I wasn't in your line of fire."

"I was shaking so hard I don't know if I could'da hit him anyway. I was glad we had a gun, but I never in a million years thought we would have to use it. Next time you hitch a ride with somebody, check their credentials! That old boy was nuts."

"When you stick your thumb out, you take what you can get. Let's just leave," Johnny replied. "This is too much excitement for one day."

"Next time we need supplies," Bill said, "I'm going. Mosquitos like to ate me alive. I lost ten pounds of blood just sittin' there guarding the boat and waiting on you."

Chapter 9
Tug Boats

The Arkansas River dumped its Oklahoma dirt and sand into the Mississippi River like a funnel, causing a streak of brown silt down the middle of the blue Mississippi waters—like the stripe on a skunk's back.

"Good grief!" Bill exclaimed. "Look at all that! We're smack-dab in the middle of an entirely new ballgame and it's too late to turn back! Gimmie a hand. We've got to shift supplies and distribute the weight or we're gonna end upside down."

The two were completely unprepared for their encounter with the waters of the Mississippi, nor had they anticipated the huge distance across it—spanning side to side from the state of Tennessee on the east to the state of Arkansas on the west.

Sitting atop their small boat, they were tiny. Insignificant. Like bugs. Floating so low in the water that they couldn't see the banks on either side of the huge river. Only when they steered the boat to the east or to the west, were they able to see land and get their bearings. Out in the middle of the river, it felt like they were adrift on an endless ocean at the mercy of the vast rushing Mississippi waters.

"Grab the tiller," Johnny screamed when they met their first tug. "Turn into his wake or we're gonna tip over!"

The Mississippi was a highway, and every few miles tug boats heading north passed them, creating a wall of water so high that Bill and Johnny had to fight to stay upright, aiming their Jonboat straight into the wake to keep from being turned over. The tugs were huge, pushing unwieldy flotillas of containers. Six containers wide and up to six containers deep—filled with products headed to St. Louis and beyond.

Every tug created a surge that lifted them up and into the wave, swamping the boat then dropping them back down on the other side with a thud—where they frantically bailed water. They had left the danger of the quicksand in the Arkansas only to face the real possibility of being run over by tugs and containers and drowning in the Mississippi.

Between their harrowing encounters with Northbound tugs, they cut the motor to conserve gasoline—and drifted. Fishing and selling their catch to Southbound tugs that didn't swamp their boat with waves.

"Pull up to the side of that tug and holler at them," Bill told Johnny. "I'll hold a big fish up so they can see what we've got."

Johnny drifted alongside the tug, and Bill reached up to the deck hands exchanging the fish they had caught for badly needed cash; supplies were costing more than they had planned on, and they were almost broke.

Tug captains and deckhands formed their own tight-knit community on the river, passing each other day in and day out heading North or headed South. News about the two Oklahoma boys floating the river was an interesting diversion for the tug crews, a novelty that interrupted the boring every-day-is-the-same for the community of tug-boat river traffic.

Captains spread the word to those who forged up and down the river; blowing their horns in greeting as they passed the two adventurers—fish mongers, selling their catch from a boat that looked like a tiny speck on the face of the mighty Mississippi River.

Chapter 10
Shanties

There was always the problem of where they would pull ashore at night and set up their cots. Sleeping in the boat hadn't worked—one of them watching and guiding their drift while the other tried to sleep. The constant problem of the tugs roiling and upsetting the water had put that idea to rest.

Occasionally, they passed small settlements. Groups of shanties, lean-tos, and tents huddled on the banks, or houseboats floating on the water.

"What do you think," Bill asked. "You think it's safe?"

"No roads in or out," Johnny replied. "Only way in is by water. No cars or trucks. Just boats and shacks. Looks like an isolated cluster of huts to me."

"It's pretty isolated," Bill said. "Looks like they depend on the river to get anywhere."

"I say we try it. Maybe they'll give us some hot food before they kill us."

Cut off from civilization, each small river colony lived by their own set of rules and their own laws. They hunted, fished, and lived off the water and land—making rare excursions out for what they couldn't produce themselves.

For the most part, the clusters of people were friendly, glad to see visitors who had no agenda—people who had no desire to tax them, rob them, or change their way of life. They welcomed the boys, showed them where to set up their cots, shared their home-grown concoction of mosquito repellant and fed them roasted wild boar grilled on a spit over an open fire.

After days of eating out of cans, the food tasted like manna, making it hard to break themselves away and get back in the boat. They gorged themselves on hot food that the small clusters of people seemed more than willing to share. Evenings were spent around a campfire swapping food in exchange for stories about the boy's adventures floating down from 'up north'.

People wanted to hear where the boys had come from, and why they were headed to the Gulf; it was an interesting and entertaining diversion for the small isolated groups. None understood why the boys would leave their homes, nor why anyone would want to float the Mississippi, much less to New Orleans. Big city life was what those isolated groups of settlers were escaping.

"Nothin' but French-Catholics, no-see'um gnats and drunks in New Orleans. All they want to do down there is baptize you, bite you, or shoot you. You two boys ought'ta turn your boat around and go home. Nothin' good go'in on in New Orleans."

After a breakfast of eggs and wild boar bacon, the rag-tag groups bid them farewell, asked them not to reveal their location to the 'law', and wished them God-speed.

"We don't need the law poking around here. We's mostly moon-shine Baptists. We ain't sprinklers; nope, we dunk 'em. Cuppa'la Holy-Rollers in the bunch, but we love 'em anyway. Ya' gets sick, we got muskee'dine wine like the apostle Paul said, for the stomik's sake."

After their first stop at one of the little towns on the river, they searched the banks for shanty boat settlements each evening, and camped out at as many of them as they could. They were in no hurry; the food was good, and the people were interesting.

They had at least four more weeks before school started and they would have to give up their vagabond existence. An existence that was growing on them, and wearing them down—all at the same time.

Eventually, six weeks after they began their journey, in bad need of a haircut and shave, sun-burned, blistered, and dirty with red speckled whelps over every inch of their bodies where they had been bitten and tortured by mosquitos, they took a bath in the Mississippi and put on clean clothes they had brought with them to wear into New Orleans.

They docked in the French Quarter, walked to town, checked into a hotel, called home, and arranged a pickup for themselves and the Jonboat as soon as someone could get there.

They were too tired to explore New Orleans, and when their ride arrived, they loaded the boat on the trailer and slept all the way home stretched out in the back of the pickup.

Bill stood in a hot shower for an hour. Once the grime was scrubbed off, he stretched out on clean sheets in a real bed on a soft mattress, fluffed up a feather pillow, and slept for most of the week before he returned to OU.

Johnny left for Dartmouth to begin his freshman year of college.

They wouldn't see each other again for thirty years.

Chapter 11
Change of Major

Like every other young man in America during the Space Age, Bill dreamed of being an astronaut. The path to getting there was a college major in aeronautical engineering—which for him only lasted one semester. Until calculus, where he was assigned to a class designing wheel struts for airplanes—designs that would never actually be used. It made the decision to change his major very easy. He wasn't going to be an astronaut if it involved calculus or brain-numbing exercises designing mindless aircraft minutia.

Anthropology was his second choice; however, after a semester of studying bones, fossils, human biology, and the physiological characteristics of homo-sapiens, he realized he had no interest in animals or humanoids that had lived in the past. What he did discover—from the anthropological experience—was that he was very much interested in the biology of the living.

"Medicine," Bill told his advisor. "I want to study medicine." He had unwittingly stumbled onto something he actually wanted to do.

"You've only been here one year and this is the third time you've changed your major," his advisor told him. "You're on a full scholarship right now, but this can't continue or we are going to discontinue your funding."

"I've decided. I'm going to become a doctor," Bill said.

Although his advisor had renewed his scholarship, finances were still a critical issue. He applied for a job to every hospital and clinic within a fifty-mile radius of his hometown with no luck at all; nothing was available. The only other possibility for free room and board was to find a job somewhere that he had family he could live with.

When his sister married Ken, Bill gained a mentor—guiding him down the straight and narrow—with only partial success. He was the only brother Bill had ever known. A Marine fighter pilot, commanding officer of a squadron stationed in Beaufort, South Carolina.

"I've applied to medical school and need a place to stay this summer," he told Ken. "There's a hospital opening near where you live and they need a scrub tech in the operating room. I wondered if I could stay with you all this summer?

"If I'm going to go to Med school, I need some hands on practice to get control of a problem I have with blood. Nurses where I've been working have kept a secret for me; they stand close by to catch me in case I faint because I get woozie at the sight of blood."

"Sure. Come on. We've got plenty of room. It'll give me a chance to pound some sense into your head. For someone as smart as you are, you can sometimes be incredibly stupid."

"I also need some advice. I want to break up with this girl I'm dating," he told Ken. "She says she's going to kill herself if I do."

"So," Ken told him. "Let her."

"You're saying I should let her kill herself?"

"Yes. Unless you want to spend the rest of your life as a hostage."

"Just like that?"

"Yep. Just like that. Don't flatter yourself. She's not going to kill herself."

"I don't want to be responsible for someone killing themselves."

"Don't ever give in to a threat, buddy. It never works out very well, and you'll always be on the losing end of a bad bargain."

After he secured the job in Beaufort, he told his folks he was going to live with his sister and Ken for the summer, packed up, left Oklahoma, and checked into his new position the following Monday—where he was scared spitless his first night on the job. It wasn't at the sight of blood; it was a ghost.

The hospital morgue was down the hall from the emergency room where Bill had been assigned to work. And since nobody in the superstitious South had any interest in visiting or disturbing a morgue, it wasn't very well monitored.

At midnight, he walked down the long hall of the hospital making rounds, checking doors to be sure everything was locked up before his shift ended. It was pitch black except for a small lamp on a desk casting shadows.

At the end of the dark hall, he opened the door to the morgue and saw that the loading dock doors were standing wide open—you could see dark Spanish moss dangling from the trees outside. Someone had forgotten to close the dock doors when they had delivered a body to the morgue that night.

Bodies that had come in that day were lying on tables covered by sheets, waiting to be picked up by the local mortuary. As he opened the hall door to the morgue and moved toward the loading dock, one of the sheets began to slowly rise over the head of one of the bodies.

He stopped, gasped for breath, and backed up. The sheet lifted and began to float, hovering. Whoever was under the sheet was trying to sit up.

"Holy crap," he yelled as he tripped over something on the floor. Stumbling, trying to get up. He was in a panic.

The sheet floated for a few seconds, then settled softly back down on the body as Bill was backing up, crawling, scrambling to escape the morgue.

It took precious minutes before he could gather his wits—before he realized that when he had opened the hall door to the morgue, a draft had swept between the hall and the open loading dock doors, allowing a breeze to ripple through the room and under the sheet, raising it up, off, and over a corpse—where it floated in the air.

He felt stupid. This was one story he wasn't going to tell anyone. He didn't believe in ghosts—at least he hadn't thought he believed in ghosts until that moment. His heart was racing. He crossed the room, locked the loading dock doors, let himself out and drove home, still shaking.

Work didn't get better. The next week, there was a banging on the emergency room door—and once more, in the middle of the night. When he looked through the door's small glass window to see what was going on, he saw a face pressed up against the glass.

He punched the buzzer, opened the door, and came face to face with a huge black man clutching his stomach with blood seeping out between his fingers. On either side of the open doors were eight other blacks who were as big or bigger than the wounded man. When Bill opened the doors, they burst in—supporting their wounded friend. They were dressed in all manner of garb, feathers, Voo-Doo markings, and painted skin; Bill was scared to death. He was surrounded by giants.

He had come from a small all-white Oklahoma burg and had no experience with the culture of people from the black population. He had been trying to learn—since Beaufort County was seventy-two percent black—and so far, he had been doing OK. When they were hurt, blacks reacted pretty much the same as white people. Scared.

He reached for the wounded man, gave him support, helped him onto a gurney, and began to roll him down the hall—followed by the wildly clad entourage. Bill had only taken a few steps when he heard an unmistakable sound. The 'Click-click-schuss' of a switch-blade.

His heart stopped. He instantly came to a halt, held his breath, and stood there motionless. Afraid to move. Waiting. Finally, slowly, he turned around, and faced a man with an open switch-blade, pointed straight at him.

"Doc," the man said, "Dis' here's da' knife what stuck 'em with—you wan' it? You needs'ta see how long was da' blade?"

"Thank you," Bill whispered. His throat was dry and he could hardly breathe. "Why don't you lay it down there on this gurney for the surgeon to examine."

Getting the blade out of the man's hands was the only thought he could muster at the moment.

In a complete panic, surrounded by black Voodoo giants, he called for the surgeon on the emergency room phone line, then asked the wounded man's friends to help lift the patient onto the operating table as he tried to stop the bleeding with his shaking hands.

When the emergency room surgeon arrived, he checked the patient for possible internal damage done by the switch-blade, declared him extremely lucky, stitched him up, and sent him and his friends packing. No charge of course.

"Do ya wanna' keep da blade?" the man who had given Bill the switch blade asked. "Hit' don't belong to none of us."

"No, you keep it; take it with you," the surgeon told him. "We've got plenty of knives around here already."

His friends lifted the wounded man off the table and assisted him to the door, thanking Bill and the surgeon profusely. "Th'ank ya', doc. 'Preciate it."

After they were gone, Bill asked, "Aren't you going to call the police?" He was still in a panic.

"Of course not. Why would I want to do that? Nothing happened around here tonight that I saw, except that you and I just made nine new friends, and who knows, we may need a little Voo-Doo someday. They'll take care of whoever and whatever needs to be taken care of. No need for anybody to involve the police; we don't want to stir up a hornet's nest. You and I don't know anything about anything. OK?"

"Yes, sir. I don't know anything about anything or anybody. I got it. But don't you wonder what happened to whoever it was that stuck him with the knife?"

"Nope. Don't really want to know. None of our business—and just so you don't misunderstand me, you and I never saw them. Those guys are from Frogmore, over on the island. They don't speak much English—they speak Getchee-Gullah. Whoever stuck the guy wasn't from the island—those are good folks over there. They mind their own business and take care of their own justice."

That night, a new sound was permanently etched in Bill's memory that he would never, ever, forget. It was the sound of a switch-blade opening. 'Click-click-schuss'.

Chapter 12
Med School

He finished course requirements for Med school during his third year of college and was immediately accepted. He never finished a college degree; it wasn't required. His exceptional entry score, top college grades, and Med school interview were his ticket to ride. The only thing he didn't have was financing. Unlike many med applicants, he didn't come from a family who had the financial resources to fund his medical school endeavor.

"What are you going to do?" his roommate Henson asked him. Henson came from an upper-class family and had no problems with financing.

"Get a job. I don't have a choice. I've been living on borrowed money, school loans, and whatever jobs I can find. Now, I have to earn some real money to pay for Med school."

The decision to switch to medicine had made a regular, ongoing, reliable job an absolute necessity—it was the only way he could continue to offset the cost. When an opening came as an orderly at a cancer research facility for children—he took it. It was dirty work cleaning up bloody operating rooms and swabbing floors in the rooms of desperately tragic patients—children who were victims of the ravages of cancer.

Outlandishly bad behaviors had gone unchecked in the ward—there were no behavioral guidelines for the young patients. None. Children were sick and dying and nobody—parents, nurses, or doctors—wanted to upset sick children by imposing rules and restrictions on them.

Bill immediately determined that his job would be impossible without cooperation from the young patients, and laid down the law—explaining to each out-of-control unruly child, "No, you can't do that here. You can't run up and down the halls. You can't pull the pic line out of your arm. You can't yell at people—unless you are hurting. If you want me to read to you or play games with you, you have to follow my rules."

As he assumed the unexpected role of resident parent, he fell in love with his work—helping children endure the nightmare imposed on them by the painful, unrelenting treatment of their disease. In return, they obeyed his rules and restrictions, responding to the behavioral boundaries he expected of them—hungry for the attention that the overworked doctors and nurses never had time to give.

The only heartbreaking part of the job as an orderly was when he had to roll a gurney through the underground tunnels beneath the facility to the morgue—with the body of a child who didn't make it. After the first three or four, he had learned how to control his tears.

Surely, there had to be better answers for this disease that killed so many children.

Chapter 13
Learning to Study

Only after he had enrolled in medical school did he realize that the choice to go to Med school presented him with an unforeseen and looming threat. A war was going on in Vietnam, and every single medical graduate was immediately sent to the war when they finished their internship. They were automatic draftees. For med students, there were no exceptions including those who were 4-F.

It may not have been fair to draft all of the medical students, but the government was doing what had to be done. They had to have doctors. And if the government drafted you—which they were going to do—you lost all of your choices as to where you were going to be assigned. You were going to go where they said you were going to go. You were going to 'Nam—to an unholy war of attrition—with a poor chance of surviving. The war was killing medics at an alarming rate.

Bill did not intend to be drafted and sent to the ground war, so he sold his soul. He signed on the dotted line, avoiding the draft by joining the Navy—who assumed his Med school expenses in exchange for four years of his life. He prayed the war would be over before he finished his medical internship.

Choosing to sign up with the Navy had seemed like the smart thing to do; he would be assigned to a ship—not to the ground war which was where all of the Army doctors were going to go. Unfortunately, it was a misguided decision. Every Marine Corps unit on the ground in Vietnam was assigned a Navy doctor. His assumption that he would be assigned to a ship had been totally wrong.

One of the short-timers—who had made it back alive after finishing his tour in Vietnam—told Bill, "Over there, you either get a Silver-Star, or you end up being court-martialed. Our unit would send us into the villages to help the people who lived there. We were unarmed—since guns are against the Geneva Convention for doctors.

"They sent medics in-country without preparing them for combat—none of us had any training at all in how to fight. None. They told us we were on a peaceful mission. They just forgot to mention that to the Viet Cong.

"The villages where we would be sent would come under attack and of course, against regulations, all of us had a gun in our black bag—the problem was managing to get to it in time to use it.

"Over and over again, we were fighting hand to hand, with knives and knuckles. One of the corpsmen working with our unit even threw himself on a hand-grenade. Killed him—saved the rest of us. He got a medal, but that doesn't do a dead man any good.

"When the attack on a village would end, the Cong would drag their military dead off into the bush—leaving us surrounded by dead civilians. We hadn't killed any civilians, but depending on who came in later to take the report and write it up, the result could go either way. We were in the middle of a sea of civilian bodies with no enemy casualties anywhere to indicate that there had been a fight. All we could do was tell the military what had happened. They either believed it, or they didn't. Like I said, we got a Silver Star or were court-martialed."

Stories like that were depressing. The part about helping villagers was uplifting, but the part about the Viet Cong definitely wasn't. Bill really didn't want to go to war. But it seemed like war was going to be an inevitable destination for him.

Chapter 14
Flunking a Test

For the first time in his life, Bill's study habits—or rather his lack of study habits—had caught up with him. He had never had to study before in his entire life and had already floated through the first year of Med school before he realized that floating wasn't going to work. This wasn't the Mississippi River. Everyone in his med classes was as smart or smarter than he was.

The school of medicine didn't have an open door. Not just anyone could apply and get in. Criteria for acceptance was in the stratosphere of mental acuity and academic achievement—a stratosphere that he had always taken for granted back in the real world. Now, he was going to have to play catch up. Big time. He was behind and was going to have to learn how to study. Or he was going to flunk out before he even got started.

On the first test in anatomy, he didn't even make the grade board. He was shocked. He had never failed a test in his life.

One of the students in his class was a grad student working on a Ph.D. in anatomy; he already knew every tiny detail of every nerve, tendon, muscle, bone, artery, and vessel in the human body—before he joined the class. On every exam, there was somebody like that who already knew it all, and set the grade curve without having to work at it—and it wasn't Bill.

Bill's test score was in the bottom fourth. He was going to be finished with Med school before he got started unless he made some changes—and made them immediately.

He paid closer attention to dissecting the cadaver he shared with three of his friends from college who were also med students: Will, Steve, and Smithy.

"I've got to learn this stuff," Bill told them. "Or I'm going to be history. Don't look for me after classes, or tempt me to go anywhere. I'm going to have my nose in a book for the rest of the semester or I'm dead in the first reader. You guys passed the first exam. I didn't."

Before the semester was over, he had made the grade. Barely. The upside was that he had finally learned how to study.

He didn't particularly like the classes in psychiatry. However, all of the psychiatry students in his class took the lessons much more seriously after an incident with one of their fellow classmates. The student had taken the restraints off of a seemingly calm patient that had been diagnosed by an attending Psychiatrist as mentally unstable and dangerous. The student paid with his life when the patient calmly reached for a pair of scissors on a side table and stabbed the med student in the chest. Killing him instantly with efficiency and no remorse.

Chapter 15
The Girl

Days in medical school. Nights in the children's cancer ward. Summer in the Navy Reserves. Exhausted all the time.

Finding a time to go home and see family was hard; Thanksgiving, Christmas, and a rare weekend were the best he could do. But on occasion, when they were home at the same time, he would see Janet at church.

She was in her third year as an art major at Kansas University, and through mutual friends, he heard she had turned down a marriage proposal. Broken up with one guy and now was seriously dating someone else.

Just like Christian in 'Pilgrim's Progress', he had fallen into the 'Slough of Despond', and couldn't seem to find his way back to the place or the person he had been before he left home for college three years earlier. He had made a lot of bad choices. None of which would make him attractive to Janet. There was no end to the number of men she could date—men who had kept their residence and lives in the same Christian world that she lived in.

She was always in the back of his mind; he thought about her. There had been women, but nothing permanent. It's hard to get interested in someone when the perfect girl might still be—out there. When there was still a chance that she might be—? Might be what? What?

When he returned home from Med school that next Christmas and went to church, he saw her in a group visiting with some of their other friends; he sat down beside her and asked how she was doing. How was school? Was she still majoring in art? He didn't hear the sermon; he was thinking about what she would say if he asked her out and decided it was worth enduring one more rejection.

When the final hymn had been sung, the benediction prayer and amen were over, he swallowed his pride and asked if she would like to go get something to eat that evening. He wasn't hopeful; his lifestyle in college hadn't earned him any status in her eyes. Word got around—he expected her to say no. She had relegated him to the guys on her 'Do-Not-Ever-Date-Again' list back when he was a freshman in high school—and there hadn't been any reason for her to change her mind about him. He didn't blame her.

She was pretty. She was smart. She was also funny with a great sense of humor. When they were in high school, they had traveled hundreds of miles together on the church bus with their youth choir, staying in parishioners' homes in the towns where they sang—so, he had spent a lot of time with her, even though she wouldn't go out with him. They were also in student council his senior year; he admired how she had been able to hold her own in a discussion and help the group resolve problems—although he had never told her so.

With all those thoughts running through his mind, he walked out of the church door at the same moment she did, and asked if she would like to go get something to eat that evening. She said no. She had previous arrangements. What did he expect? The last time he had a date with her, he had forgotten it.

But as he was about to say goodbye, she said, "I'm going to see the Messiah in Tulsa this evening. Would you like to go with me?"

He was so shocked that the only reply he could come up with was, "Yes."

"Pick me up at four if you want to have time to go get something to eat."

"Four?"

"Yes, four."

"OK. At four."

Stupid. Stupid; he couldn't seem to find any intelligent words.

When he got back home, he set an alarm. He wasn't going to mess up his opportunity a second time.

Reaching for her elbow as he helped her in the car, steadying her arm as they climbed the stairs to the auditorium, helping her remove her coat as they found their seat. Before the evening was over, he had touched her multiple times and couldn't help but think, "I could get used to this."

But he wasn't stupid. Reaching for her hand would raise touching to an entirely new and different level.

Halfway through the performance he asked himself, "What do I have to lose? I'm probably already dead in the water with her anyway."

He reached across the seat and took her hand.

She didn't pull away.

The next few months, if they were home at the same time, they spent time together. He drove to Kansas when he could. She drove to OU once as well. Everything seemed to be going in the right direction, and after he settled into a comfort zone conversing with her, he shared a funny story about Oklahoma's new Miss America.

She had picked him out of a lineup in a school annual, asking a mutual friend if Bill would serve as her escort to an event she had to attend. He said he would—then forgot the date.

"You see," Bill told Janet. "When I forgot our date, it was never you. It was me. I'm the problem. You and Miss America both proved that it's me. I'm absent-minded. The two best-looking girls in America got stood up by the same stupid dope."

To Bill, it seemed that whatever differences they had stumbled over in the past were just that. In the past. He was glad those things were behind them.

Finally, one afternoon over Spring Break when they were both home, walking hand in hand in the city park, he said, "I need to share something with you. The truth is—this is not a good time for me to fall in love—I'm headed back to medical school in the fall. I don't have time to be in love. But I am. I'm in love with you. I think I always have been. As soon as I finish Med school, would you marry me?"

He was confident at this point in their relationship that she would say yes. Which was not the answer he got.

"No. I'm not getting married. To you, or anyone else. I'm leaving in a few months to go to China," she told him. "My assignment there is for a single person. I'll be there for two years."

"China? What do you mean you're going to China? What assignment?" He was stunned. "What are you talking about? When did you decide to do this? Why haven't you mentioned this to me before now? You're going to just up and go to China—just like that! Out of the blue!"

"It's not out of the blue," she said. "I've been thinking about this for a long time. Over a year. I flew to Dallas a week ago and made arrangements to leave the states in a few months."

"Why haven't I heard about this before now!"

"We've had no words of commitment. You never said you loved me. I never said I loved you. We've never even talked about a future together. I'm graduating college in two months. You have to finish medical school. I didn't see any point in sitting around waiting for another year or two just to see where this was going. You've given me no indication until right now that you wanted something permanent.

"I decided I wanted to go to China last year. We had a guest speaker at the Baptist Student Union who told us about a program for singles—two years on the mission field, salaried, housing, and working for the Baptist International Mission Board. The IMB.

"It sounded like something I would enjoy doing. They match you up with a job overseas somewhere. Sometimes you replace missionaries who are returning to the states on furlough. They have assignments all over the world; I signed up and chose Hong Kong. I'll be working for the Hong Kong Baptist Press for the next two years as an artist."

He was stunned. This was not what he had been expecting at all. She had said no. No! He was crushed.

Chapter 16
Stayin' Alive

"What'cha got planned for the summer?" Bill had called Will Henson—his college roommate. They were not only roommates but best friends; both of them were headed back to medical school in the fall.

"I know this guy who lives in California," Henson said. "He told me to come out there for the summer and work with him in a packaging plant. What do you have going on?"

"Well, I was obviously overconfident about…well, I had it in my head to get married. But she said no; so that settles that. I'm loose." Bill continued, "Which is a good thing. I couldn't get married anyway—I've got no money."

"What were you thinking! You aren't ready to get married."

"Who said I was thinking? Anyway, I've been home for a week and my parents are already sick of me."

"Same here. They love me better when I'm someplace else."

"So—you're actually going to go to California? You think I could get a job there too? I'm broke. Busted. California sounds good to me."

"Let's go. I've got a car. It's got a hundred and sixty thousand miles on it, but I think it might make it," Henson said.

"I'm in," Bill told him. "Can we charge the gas—split the bill when I get back to my job in the fall?"

"Can't charge much, my card is maxed out, and I bet yours is too. We'll have to work for gas. But it sounds like a plan. I'll pick you up tomorrow."

The car made it. The plans for a job didn't. Every job in San Francisco was unionized—even the paper boys. And neither one of them had a union card.

They were up a creek without a paddle and the car was going to soon be running on fumes. The only place in San Francisco they could find to live that they could afford—was a one room dump over the Chucker bar that got raided by the police every night. After a couple of nights, they understood why the rent was so low.

"I keep getting propositioned," Henson told Bill. "Did you notice that everybody in this building is queer as a duck? We'd probably be better off sleeping on the beach. Or in the car? I can sleep on sand if you can. We need to check out of here and spend what money we have left on food. Rod's Frontier Cafeteria has all-you-can-eat for a dollar a day. But if we don't find some kind of work, we're going to run out of money."

"Only way I've found to get quick cash is to sell blood. Use blood money for gas and keep looking for some kind of work to do," Bill added.

The nurse at the Red Cross donation center took their blood and gave them a tip. "Years ago, when my husband was going to college, he sold encyclopedias to make money. Maybe you boys could do that."

The job required that they attend an encyclopedia convention in Los Angeles. They hitched a ride from San Francisco to L.A. and stayed at the meeting long enough to get bored and start walking back to their hotel. Through Watts. They had no idea where they were. Two ignorant Okies who didn't know the territory.

It didn't take very long for them to be surrounded by six huge guys with Afros and doo-rags who began pushing them into each other, taunting them—obviously in control of the situation.

"What's a couple of white boys doin' on our streets?" one of them asked. Bill and Will were trapped, defenseless, and scared to death. The Doo-rags began to push them into each other in earnest, poking and threatening them.

At that moment, two white girls in a convertible slowed down next to them and screamed, "Get in!"

The boys flew over the side of the convertible into the back seat, tires screeching as they pulled out.

"What are you two guys doing down here! You must have a raging case of stupid. Are you nuts? This is Watts. This is their territory; they own these streets! You have no business here—you could have been killed!"

"What are you two white girls doing here in the middle of the night? That's the real question," Bill asked them. He was still shaking—and Will had turned an even whiter shade of white. "We're not from here. We didn't know we had broken some unwritten code until it was too late. God himself must have sent you."

The girls let them off at their hotel, promising to check on them the next day.

They never saw the girls again. "Those two girls were angels," Bill told Henson. "The Bible says something about meeting angels and being unaware of it. I think they were angels."

"I don't believe in angels," Henson replied. "You're the Bible thumpin' guy."

One week later, riots broke out in Watts, involving 34,000 people. There were 34 killed, 1032 injured, and 4000 arrests. Over one thousand buildings were completely destroyed; there were forty million dollars in damages, tearing the fabric of Los Angeles apart.

"You read the paper?" Bill asked Will. "You change your mind about angels? That's who we met the other night—whether you believe in angels or not. We were walking down the street in the middle of an emerging war zone and we didn't even know it."

By the end of one week knocking on doors, it was obvious that nobody bought encyclopedias anymore—and the two were desperate. Their blood money was running out.

And that wasn't the only problem they faced. The encyclopedia salesman that Bill had been assigned to work with was nuts. He kept a forty-five under the front driver's seat along with a three-foot length of chain. Every time anybody drove by and looked at him sideways, he jumped out of the car and started breaking their car windows with the chain, waving the gun around in the air.

"I'm going to end up in jail if I keep working with this guy," Bill told Henson. "He's crazy as a loon. We've got to find something else to do pretty soon, or go home."

"How are we gonna get home," Will asked. "We don't have any money for gas and I'm running out of blood. This is not a good situation."

"I don't know, but I'm done with encyclopedias. Let's sleep on the beach; it's free. We need to try surfing before we crash and burn anyway. It may be our last chance to give it a try and see if we can do it."

"You got to be kidding. I'm not surfing. Sharks, drowning, and all that. You surf. I'll watch the girls in bikinis."

They parked the car on the beach, used their last five dollars, and rented Bill a surfboard. Livin' in the moment. Flat broke, almost out of gas, and had no idea where their next meal was coming from.

Cute girls were everywhere, lying on bright-colored beach towels, next to ice chests packed full of sandwiches, and Colas. It took all of five minutes for the 'Will and Bill' duo to find a couple of cute beach bunnies who were willing to share their food and blankets. The fact that both of them were good-looking had its advantages.

"Guard the stuff in those girl's ice chests while I go surf," Bill told Henson. "But keep an eye on me as well."

"You ever surfed before?" Will asked him.

"Never. That's why I want you to watch. It can't be that hard. If I get in trouble, come get me."

"Will do." Which he didn't.

Bill was in trouble when the first crest upended the board and threw him into the air. He came down head first, and couldn't get out of the pounding waves. The ocean sucked him under and within minutes he lost all strength to fight the surge; he realized that he wasn't going to make it. Desperation overtook him. He had nothing left to fight the sucking rip tide; he had no choice but to give up, and when he did, the waves took him.

He had passed just being in trouble, he was drowning, and nobody was coming to help. "This is it," he thought. And at that moment, his toe brushed sand and he realized that there was hope beneath him. He struggled to upend himself and get his footing with every ounce of draining strength that he had left. Digging a foot into the sand, he raised his head above the waves, caught his breath, and dragged himself to shore—where Will was nonchalantly entertaining a crowd of cute girls.

"Where were you! Why didn't you come to help me!" he screamed at Will.

"What are you talking about? I didn't know you had started to surf. You didn't come tell me you got your board in the water yet."

"I coulda' died out there and you're chasing beach bunnies," Bill yelled at him.

"Sorry, buddy. Hey! It turned out OK, you're alive, and I found us some cute beachies who've got food! And one of them let me siphon some gas out of her car."

They finished off most of the accommodating girl's sandwiches and crammed the rest into a tote. Will threw it over his shoulder without asking the beachies if he could take it. Bill picked up as many of the girl's Pepsis as he could carry and the two boys waved goodbye, piled into the car, and headed for Lake Tahoe to look for work. California hadn't panned out.

They made Tahoe, barely. At midnight, the car sputtered a couple of times, ran out of gas, and came to a halt. They coasted into Harrah's parking lot and fell asleep in the car.

The next morning, unpresentable, dirty and still covered with beach sand, they found a hydrant at the back of the building, washed themselves off, and combed their hair. Reasonably cleaned up, they headed to the application office looking for someone in charge of hiring.

"We both need a job," Bill told the manager. "We'll do whatever you need done—we're flat broke and our car is out of gas. We got nothing to offer but attitude and energy."

"That's the very thing I happen to need around here," the manager replied. "You're hired. We need fellas to follow a couple of famous guys around who like to play the slots. They refuse to carry anything but bills in their pockets—but they need coins to play. I need someone to keep people at a distance and hop and fetch for them. Keep them supplied with quarters. Your job is to change their paper into coins, stand nearby and keep the fans at bay. Fans tend to swarm them."

"OK. We can do that. What do we do when we run out of coins? Where do we trade in the paper?"

"The cashier. Main desk. Work in tandem so that one of you is always on the spot—the other one can trade the paper in and keep a supply of coins going.

"Bill, I'm assigning you to Jack Benny. Believe it or not, he purchased his own personal slot machine and had us set it up; one that takes pennies. He's tight as a tick."

The manager assigned Will to Danny Thomas, and the two boys proceeded to follow the stars around.

Jack and Danny headed to the cafeteria each day at lunchtime, talking to the boys while the four of them ate. Being famous had its serious drawbacks. Getting away from fans to have a normal conversation over a bite to eat was one of them, and lunch had become a pleasant interlude each day at noon. The two stars got a kick out of hearing the boy's escapades—especially Bill's description of floating down the Mississippi—and how he had handled the Associated Press at Dardanelle.

"I'll tell you what," Benny told him. "If you want the job, I'll hire you full-time to get rid of the press for me. Sounds like you know how to make them back off."

"Thank you, but no thank you, sir; I don't want to mess with the press. We're heading east, back to Oklahoma, as soon as we have enough money to cover the gas to get there. We're both returning to Med school in the fall."

Within a couple of weeks, the duo had earned enough to fund their trip home. They thanked Harrah's manager for the work, thanked their famous new friends for the lunchtime conversations, and left Lake Tahoe behind. Glad to be leaving. Fame and the big lights weren't all that appealing underneath the glitter.

Chapter 17
NASA

After school the following summer, the Navy assigned Bill to NASA to work as a comparison control. A human Doppel-ganger for Gus Grissom. Everything Grissom did, Bill replicated—in exactly the same order and motion.

That summer of 1966, NASA had assigned every astronaut a double—someone who knew absolutely nothing about aviation, someone that could give NASA an unbiased human duplicate control for each individual astronaut as they did their experimental tests. Someone to compare the things an astronaut was capable of doing—against what a regular untrained human would do. How an astronaut would react in an experiment, measured against how their control would react in the same situation. There was no explanation as to why they were doing what they were doing; they just were. Government mentality at its finest.

The Naval Aerospace Medical Institute, or NAMI as it was commonly called, was located in Pensacola, Florida. By changing his major to medicine, Bill realized that he wasn't going to become an astronaut, but he was finally going to NASA—as a guinea pig, assigned to replicate the tests that were being performed on an astronaut.

He took his turn in the centrifuge seated in a cab at the end of a long steel arm—subjected to continually increasing rotational speed—spinning, pulling G forces. Accelerating throughout the test until he either threw up or passed out.

NASA was always coming up with new experiments to try. They basically had no idea what space was going to do to a human body, and they were trying to find out. Blood pressure tests, zero gravity tests, tests to find out how a person's balance was affected by pressure changes in the inner ear.

One experiment put him inside a ball that was inside a ball—inside another ball. Three balls nested like Russian Dolls—stacked inside each other. The monitor spun the inner ball in one direction, the middle ball in the opposite direction, and the outside ball head over heels. The balls were constructed of clear, see-through materials so that the test monitor could watch the man seated inside—who was blindfolded and trying to use his controls to stop rotation of all three balls at once. Simulating an experience that might occur in space where there was no point of reference.

Another test placed the guinea-pig-control-double in a furnished roundhouse that had no corners. When the structure began to rotate, the monitor would record the control's ability to stand up straight, bend or tilt their head. When the control had adjusted to the constant spinning, the monitor would toss a ball onto the floor, which would roll in a curve and not in a straight line—It was extremely disorienting. By the time the control left the trial after a week of living in a rotating house—he couldn't stand up straight for hours. Sometimes days.

Bill only lasted one day as a control in that particular test. Nausea, disorientation, and inability to stand or walk knocked most of the human guinea pigs out of the experiment. When you were sitting still in a chair inside the house, you couldn't tell you were moving. But standing and walking in the rotating house was a different thing. Much like getting adjusted to the roll and pitch of a carrier—where you felt you were in motion only after you got off the ship.

At one point, NASA considered putting sailors into the astronaut pipeline. When the sailors had taken their enlistment medical exams, it was discovered that some of them were labyrinth defective. Due to a defective inner ear—they didn't get dizzy. NASA subsequently transferred them to Pensacola to use them as additional guinea pigs. The sailors were able to stay in the spinning balls and walk around in the rotating roundhouse—it didn't affect them at all. They had no problems with it, never lost their balance, and could step out of the test seven days later and walk in a straight line.

NASA also had a top-secret lab underground. It was deceptive. One story, no windows, with hidden stairs inside that went down, down, down to the actual lab—where there were state-of-the-art simulators. Dome screens for three-dimensional effects. Used for training on how to fly a spacecraft with no reference point other than a dot in the distance. Bill tried his hand flying toward the tiny dot, and couldn't do it. He was not alone.

The questions were endless. How would a person live without gravity? What would months of living in a spinning environment do to your blood volume, your blood pressure, and a million other unanswered questions.

There were tests for mental and emotional degeneration. What would happen out there to your mind? One test for mental cognizance was to give them a random series of numbers, spin them until they passed out, then have them repeat the numeral sequence.

Nobody had gone to space before. Nobody knew the answers to those questions, and there were millions of unanswered questions.

NASA was pushing preparation for the first space station. Apollo 1. Which was projected for the next January. John Glenn orbited the earth in February 1962. And in the summer of 1966, when Bill was assigned his work as a control, NASA was still trying to figure out the effects of space on the human body.

Several teams, each consisting of four astronauts, were ready to go. If for some reason one team couldn't make it, there was another team of four waiting in the wings. There were even backups for the backups.

Each member of Bill's team of four astronauts were ready to go into space the following January, not knowing which of them would be the final three chosen, and which one would be back up. Grissom, White, and Chaffee were picked and were sitting inside the spacecraft—when an electrical spark turned the Apollo One capsule into an instant inferno. Carpenter survived because he had been chosen as backup that day.

The news feed read:
CAPE KENNEDY—Friday night, America's first three Apollo astronauts died only 218 feet off the ground in a blazing explosion inside their space capsule atop its launch pad. January 27, 1967.

Those three deaths dealt the nation's moon exploration program a serious setback. The men's names had been household words in America, as the entire world watched and waited. NASA and the nation were stunned by the fatal incident; there wouldn't be another try for several more years.

Bill had now encountered his first experience with death in the Navy. The team of astronauts he had worked with were the first deaths that personally touched him—but there would be dozens and dozens of more deaths for him to deal with in the future.

After the tragedy, on weekends, after spending all day in the disorienting tests that NASA was subjecting him to, he needed a diversion. A top-secret Navy Demolition Team were using their acquired skills to make extra money on weekends by teaching scuba to anyone who wanted to learn. They certified you, and members of the team put you through the same training the Navy Demolition Team was going through.

Bill paid his money, took his chances, and learned how to scuba—which was exciting, frightening, dangerous, and a lot of fun. The gulf water of the Pensacola beach offered a calming retreat. White sand, rippling waves, clean blue water. An escape from the grueling NASA tests.

Later, the Navy Demo Team that taught Bill to scuba was given a new name. Navy Seals.

Chapter 18
China Doll

He had written letters to her during his last year of medical school—never giving up hope that maybe, someday, when she came home from Hong Kong, she would reconsider his offer.

"I've been in surgery all day," he wrote. "They let me close an incision for the first time. The attending physician said that next time, I'll get to open—hopefully. It depends on who the attending physician is. Some of them try to teach you something; some of them don't. Those that don't, expect you to watch and learn how to do it without touching anything—which isn't possible. Cutting is a lot different than watching someone else cut."

"I've been drawing pictures of Chinese children today," she answered. "They are playing some kind of game with small stones. I haven't figured the game out yet. I'm trying, but they laugh at me when I ask if I can have another turn. One good thing has come from it, I'm learning the language by listening to them talk to each other."

"Last week, I delivered babies," he wrote. "Six babies a day most days. Staff leaves you alone to deliver them by yourself—unless something goes wrong, then every resident on the floor wants in on it. Residents have no interest in the ordinary cases. They just supervise. We senior med students take care of ordinary."

"Have you kept count of how many boys and how many girls you've delivered?"

"No, I just hand the baby off to a nurse while I take care of the mother—and then they roll the next one in. They are pretty much lined up, one after another all day and all night. We trade off the nights. I don't know how many babies the others have delivered. I've had a number of forty-eight-hour shifts without relief. What have you been doing that's new?"

"I finished illustrating all the Bible School material for Chinese churches this week. They'll use them in Chinese churches scattered all over the world this summer—when children are out of school. Painting the illustrations took some doing; there are subtle differences in the color and style of the clothing they wear over here—in contrast to what kids are wearing in the states."

"I'm going home next week for a few days," Bill said. "The Navy is giving some of us a break. Thanksgiving or a couple of days at Christmas—one or the other because the hospital has to stay staffed. Mom told me your folks call you once a month. If I'm in town when that happens, maybe I'll get to talk to you."

Chapter 19
Second Proposal

"I wondered if I could come over this evening when you call Janet," Bill asked her parents. He had gone to church that morning and had taken a seat in the pew adjoining them.

"Sure," Mr. Morgan said. "We'll make the call tonight when she is awake—there's a thirteen-hour difference in time between Oklahoma and Hong Kong."

"Tell me when, and I'll be at your house."

"Did she tell you that we're going to meet her in Europe as soon as she finishes her tour in Hong Kong?" Mr. Morgan asked. "We're going to stay a month, see the sights, then go to Wales where I grew up. I'm excited about it. I haven't ever been back, and I'm hoping some of the people I knew back then are still there."

"She told me you were meeting her in Europe. It sounded like she's looking forward to visiting where you were born and grew up."

"We're anxious. It's been a long two years since she left. I'll give you a call and let you know when we get ready to phone her tonight."

Bill had tried to call her a few times with no luck at all. She had no phone at her apartment, and both of their work schedules made connecting almost impossible. He had to write her to tell her the time he would call so that she would be near a phone at work—and invariably there would be an emergency at the hospital and he couldn't get to a phone.

Nine o'clock that evening he drove over to the Morgan's house and knocked at the door. Janet's mother Delia answered, and told him to come in. "We're getting ready to call Janet."

"That's why I'm here. I'm hoping you'll give me a minute to speak to her. I haven't had any luck getting through to her at all. Every time I set up a plan to phone, we've had an emergency at work. And the three to five-day delay between letters before we can set up another time has made it almost impossible to connect. It wouldn't be so difficult if I had a regular schedule. But I don't. I have no control over my time. I never know what the next minute will be. Or the next emergency that will come in the door."

When the Morgans dialed the work number at the Baptist Press, Bill went into the kitchen and drank a cup of coffee. He thought about what he was going to say to her, and how he was going to say it. He was nervous.

After a bit, Hugh called through the kitchen door, "We're done talking if you want a minute or two."

Bill picked up the phone, said hello, then said what he had planned beforehand that he was going to say. "You're going to be through in Hong Kong in a few months. I'm done with Med school, and as soon as I finish my internship, I hope to go to flight school. That's what my plan is, but the important thing is that you know I love you. So—when you come home, will you marry me?"

There was a long pause before she answered. "I've met someone here. I've been thinking about what I want for my future—and right now, I'm unprepared for your question. I don't know how I feel or what I want. I've been thinking that I may want to live the rest of my life in China."

"China? You've met someone there?"

"I don't know how to answer you right now. I haven't seen you in two years. I didn't know I would be talking to you tonight when my folks called. I had no idea you were going to ask me to marry you and I can't clear my head right this minute. I'll write to you."

Chapter 20
China

The summer Bill spent in California, Janet was in Virginia for two months of mission orientation before leaving for Hong Kong—where she had been assigned to work with the Hong Kong Baptist Press.

Immediately, she was immersed in a strange language, strange culture, and strange foods. Thousands of miles away from anyone she knew. Transition was eased when she received an invitation from Jaxie Short to stay with her until she found an apartment. Jaxie was an older missionary from Shawnee, Oklahoma and it was comforting to meet someone from her home state.

After a couple of weeks, she relocated to an apartment with two other girls on Boundary Street. They explored the city on red double-decker British buses; they went swimming on the beach. Hong Kong consisted of more than two hundred and fifty three islands—most of them deserted—with extensive shorelines for the girls to explore.

They had no TV; however, a missionary doctor and his wife adopted them, extending a standing invitation for Friday night TV and ice cream. Hong Kong had only one English TV channel, and only one ice cream vendor—since most Chinese were lactose intolerant.

Three stray and cautious cats scoped out her apartment, decided it was safe, and adopted her; keeping the rat population at bay. She named them Shirley, Goodness, and Mercy—invoking a heavenly blessing on her new Chinese home away from home.

She walked the three blocks to work each day, soaking up the culture, encountering the people, and learning enough language to survive. Adapting to Chinese customs, dress, and food was easier than she had thought it would be.

Her assignment at work was to change or recreate the artwork in religious publications—which depicted children as white, blond, and blue-eyed. She painted scenes of Chinese children with dark black hair and distinctive eyes, wearing school uniforms and eating meals with chopsticks. Their homes, food, transportation, and lifestyles presented dozens and dozens of differences that needed to be redone and distributed to over a hundred Chinese churches around the world. Christian literature had no Christian artwork that remotely represented life in the Orient. She set about changing that. For the better.

Chapter 21
The Red Guard

Aside from the prolific rats that seemed to live in every nook and cranny of the city, the most difficult and frightening problem occurred on the streets of Hong Kong where bombs regularly exploded. The year was 1966. Mao Tse Tung's Chinese Cultural Revolution was raging inside of China and had boiled over into the area where she lived—which was now a very dangerous place to be.

That year, thousands of rag-tag young people on the Chinese mainland had sworn allegiance to Mao and formed an independent organization called the Red Guard. Mao had given that unofficial youth army their marching orders: return China to its rural economy—which the Red Guard interpreted as destroying all signs of intellectualism.

They ran rampant across China. Professionals were killed. Teachers were killed. Anyone who wore glasses was deemed to be a professional or a teacher and was subject to death. Artwork was destroyed. Slash and burn became the Red Guard's mantra. Get rid of the educated population and what is left will be acceptably rural.

Mao had not anticipated losing complete control of the Red Guard. They had run amok, extended their murderous outreach, and overrun Chinese borders into Macau—killing Christians along with the educated population. Portuguese Macau was helpless to defend themselves; they had no resources to protect or defend their territory.

Once Macau fell, the out-of-control Red Guard began an assault on British Hong Kong. Which turned out to be a 'Bridge Too Far'. Macau and the Portuguese were one thing, Hong Kong and the British were another. Britain had a one-hundred-year lease they had signed with China in 1897, during the Opium Wars—back when the British were the world's greatest naval force.

But even though Britain still had the ships and the power, the Red Guard plunged ahead, determined to take back all of the British territory of Hong Kong—and they were prepared to take it by force. Which included bombing the city's streets and buildings.

Mao was faced with a dilemma. He didn't actually want Hong Kong back—it was the export and banking center for all of China. Everything they sold had to go through the port in Hong Kong—since China had no trade agreements with the rest of the world. The term, 'Made in China' did not exist. 'Made in Hong Kong' did.

All Chinese goods had to be relabeled and exported through Hong Kong—which had the only deep-water port. That port lay between Victoria Island and Kowloon peninsula—and was under Great Britain's control. In addition to the port, the British controlled all of the two hundred and fifty three islands that made up Hong Kong.

To solve the problem of the rampant Red Guard, Mao commissioned his Chinese Red Army to take control of the young upstart Red Guard members and eliminate them—before Britain could retaliate against the unauthorized invasion and hold China responsible.

In 1966, news coming from inside China was nonexistent. What the outside world didn't know until years later was that the Red Army had not only stopped the Red Guard invasion of Hong Kong, but they had also taken control of the Chinese government itself. Mao was done. Even though he remained a figurehead, the Red Army now controlled the country—and generals took charge of every committee and institution of the nation.

As the bombing in Hong Kong stopped, missionary life returned to more peaceful and less frightening conditions. Janet had spent two years as a journeyman in the middle of a revolution that the rest of the world didn't know much about. As a foreign missionary in Hong Kong, she could have returned home to America and escaped the danger. She didn't. Those who knew her well weren't surprised at all.

Chapter 22
The Opium Wars

Her education concerning China surpassed the limited knowledge of most of America and the rest of the world, but it took the entire first year she was there to figure out enough of China's history so that she could understand why the Red Guard was bombing Hong Kong that year.

That history began in the 1800s when China would only accept silver as payment for their exceptional tea—tea that the British had become extremely fond of, and were willing to pay for. But as Britain's stores of silver began vanishing into the hands of the Chinese, the Queen was not happy and was determined to get her silver back—which meant the British needed to develop a product that China wanted to buy and pay for with silver.

The solution to the problem was simple. Create Chinese addiction for the only commodity that the British had to sell. Opium from India—a country under British control. It didn't take very long. As soon as the Chinese people developed an addiction to a British flood of opium at cheap prices, the price was raised, and silver began to flow back into the Queen's treasury. Which pleased her very much. But it caused a military conflict.

Opium Wars over silver were the result; the British moved their gunboats up the Pearl River. China had no defense, and as a concession, the British gained control of the deep-water port in Hong Kong and control of everything else up to Boundary Street. In 1897, China leased all of the territory north of Boundary Street to the British for the next one hundred years—until 1997. That treaty with the Chinese supposedly granted the British perpetuity. With sovereignty. Which didn't last.

Janet's apartment on Boundary Street was located on the edge of history. She had survived the Red Guard's invasion of Hong Kong where missionaries in Hong Kong had been high on the Red Guard list for annihilation. None of the missionaries fled the islands. They stayed put.

The chaos created by the invasion presented an opportunity for Janet to start a Bible class to support Chinese converts—since no one in the government at the time was checking what was going on with the upstart Christians. By the time the Red Army permanently removed the Red Guard, Christianity had a toe-hold.

Bill hadn't given up his pursuit of the independent, strong-willed, adventurous girl. On Valentine's Day, he went to a local florist and sent a wire to Hong Kong for a dozen roses. And since Chinese florists didn't stock roses, they changed the order to other flowers which—due to the favorable exchange rate—filled her entire apartment to overflowing, including dozens and dozens of orchids. Not knowing the exchange rate worked in his favor; it turned out much better than he had planned.

He hadn't given up hope.

Chapter 23
Ghetto Life

The last year of Med school was grueling. One foot in front of the other grueling. Med Schools were usually located in slums or other undesirable places with low income and high crime. Murder, robbery, and break-ins. It's the perfect environment for supplying medical schools with a high caseload of poor, indigent, can't-pay-for-medical-services human beings—on which med students can practice. Perfect, except for the inexperience of the medical students—which doesn't always provide the desired outcome. Free medical care does have its complications.

Bill and his friend Henson shared a two room 'suite', in a converted motel complex close to the school where they were able to walk to work—like most students who couldn't afford anything else. The complex housed dozens and dozens of nurses and med students because rent was dirt cheap. But there were shootings in the neighborhood at least once a week, and break-ins on a regular basis. There were drugs, and people passed out on the sidewalks. Gunfire at night.

One of Will and Bill's married friends was so worried about leaving his wife at home by herself that he bought her a gun. Which she used one night when someone broke into their house; she shot and killed him before he got through the door.

The police came and explained that it would be easier on them—if that ever happened again—if she would wait and shoot the perp after he got inside the house. Or if she couldn't do that, "Before you call us, drag the body through the door so we can write it up as a break and enter. Less paperwork." There was so much crime in the housing project that police were overwhelmed.

Every day on the hospital floor presented a new level of crazy. Third-year and senior med students worked the wards. If they got into trouble over their heads, they could call a resident—who might call an attending physician if necessary. No student wanted to incur the wrath of the resident by upstreaming a problem in the middle of the night—so right or wrong, they made every effort to take care of all nighttime problems in the wards themselves.

Bill got his share. At three one morning, dead on his feet from being up two nights in a row, he encountered a crazed patient running naked down the hall toward him, with a bevy of nurses trying to catch the man. Blood was spewing from where he had ripped a catheter out and torn his prostate. He was carrying a glass IV bottle with a broken tube still attached and dangling from his arm.

The patient had talked a nurse into unstrapping his ankle and wrist restraints because they were hurting him—which should have given the nurse pause to ask why he was strapped down in the first place. She didn't ask; which was a big mistake. He was loose at that point—hallucinating and running wild, screaming and cursing.

The immediate problem was to catch him, restrain him again, and stop the bleeding. But the nurses who were chasing him seemed to be concerned only with the fact that the patient was naked. They were chasing the man and trying to put a robe on him.

Orderlies and security had not yet arrived; Bill was the only thing between the hysterical patient and the outside door. He recalled something he had learned in his psychiatry classes about the fact that white medical coats could escalate problems with crazed patients, so he threw his white lab coat into a trash can and sat down calmly on the floor in the middle of the hospital corridor.

When the man came roaring down the hall toward him, Bill called to him, "Hey, John. Where are you going?"

The man stopped, confused, looked at Bill, and answered, "I've got to catch a train to Poteau."

"Oh," Bill answered, "The train's not here yet. I'm waiting on it myself. Why don't we sit here and we'll wait for it together?"

The man sat down beside Bill. "How much longer till it gets here?" he asked.

"Not long," Bill replied. Then added, "Did you know your arm is bleeding? I know how to fix that if you want me to?"

The man looked at his arm, saw the IV dangling with blood spurting everywhere, and lifted the arm up for Bill. "OK," the man said—and quietly held up his arm for Bill to tend to it.

Bill removed the IV from the patient's arm and put his thumb on the wound to stop the blood.

By that time, orderlies had arrived with a mattress. When the patient saw them, he jumped to his feet, ready to fight, yelling that he had to catch the train to Poteau. The orderlies slowly backed the man up, pinned him against a wall with the mattress, returned him to his bed, and put him back in ankle and wrist restraints.

"Don't worry," one of orderlies told the crazed patient. "The engineer on the train to Poteau said to tell you that he'll stop and pick you up later when you are better. The guy in the hall that was waiting with you for the train said to tell you he'll make sure you get on board."

Bill picked himself up off the floor, put his lab coat back on, explained the error of her ways to the nurse who had unstrapped the patient's restraints, and headed to an office to fill out paperwork.

Paperwork was always the worst part of every incident.

On the other hand, he was thankful for the hours he had spent studying with one of the Med school physicians in psychiatry. That particular doctor had raked in federal grants on a regular basis, and to appease him, the school had required all students to take his classes. Bill had hated it. So did almost everyone else. But day after day listening to instructions on how to deal with psychotic patients had finally paid off. Take your white lab coat off. Be calm. Listen more than you talk.

He had to admit that offering to get on the train to Poteau with a deranged patient was his own inventive application of what he had learned, and it helped that he was familiar with the town of Poteau. He had been assigned there as a senior medical student and had worked in the hospital for two months one summer. Twenty-four hours a day, seven days a week, he was a virtual slave to the hospital physicians. He spent every night covering the emergency room and every day following doctors around.

One of the physicians promised Bill an afternoon off to go skeet shooting with him. Bill hadn't had a break for weeks, and it sounded like fun. But after he got a couple of shots off at the clay pigeons, the doctor put him to work vaccinating cattle on his farm for the rest of the day. Free labor.

One night in the emergency room, a big burley coal miner brought his three-year-old daughter in, needing stitches for a gash under her chin. Bill asked the man if he would hold his daughter while he stitched—or should Bill page a nurse?

"Hey, nothin' bothers me. I've pulled men who were crushed out of the coal mine when we've had an accident," the man bragged. "Coupa'la stitches is nothing compared to that."

"Well, if you're OK with it, then you hold her so she doesn't move while I sew her up," Bill told him.

Bill had only taken one stitch in the young girl when her father fainted and hit his head on the floor. He was out cold. Bill called the nurse, finished stitching up the little girl—who behaved like a trooper—and then took five stitches in her father's head.

Chapter 24
Internship

At the end of the year, after graduating from Med school, he was put on active duty with the Navy—who were collecting their end of the Med school financing bargain he had signed with them. His orders were to report to Portsmouth, Virginia, and begin his medical internship. Twelve months divided into four categories. Internal Medicine, Pediatrics, Ob-Gyn, and Surgery.

Pediatrics covered every aspect of working with babies and children—who couldn't tell you what was wrong with them. Trying to make a diagnosis based on what their mother told you. He spent three months working with children whose diseases, injuries and treatment ran the gamut of the medical spectrum, sometimes not knowing if he was actually treating what was really wrong with them.

Ob-Gyn was exhausting. It seemed like every family in the military had decided to have a baby—probably because a war was on and people were being drafted, getting married, and starting families during their time in the service—where delivery and hospitalization were free. Bill delivered three-hundred and sixty babies in three months.

There were two breaches—which residents would have commandeered if they had caught them on x-ray ahead of time. Residents had first choice; they took the interesting deliveries or anything that looked like it was going to be a special case, like twins. Residents did the Cesarean sections, surgeries, hysterectomies, and cancer cases. Interns like Bill delivered babies. And babies. And more babies.

The only real conflict between the interns was over the charts—who got which case. Everyone wanted the ones marked GLM. Those represented a good-looking-mother.

One delivery turned into an unexpected and critical emergency with blood gushing everywhere; the mother was bleeding out. Bill began screaming at the top of his lungs for help. One of the residents rushed in, grabbed a scapula, and opened the mother up without time for anesthetic. He handed the baby to Bill who did CPR, trying to keep the oxygen-deprived baby alive. By some miracle, both mother and baby survived—which was not the usual outcome for a placenta previa. If someone hadn't heard him yelling for help, the mother, the baby, or both of them would have died.

The last six weeks of Ob-Gyn were spent in clinic or surgery—teamed up with a resident physician who was specializing in the field. The clinic was located in a building set apart from the Portsmouth hospital. An old, four-story structure—constructed with stones excavated from the Portsmouth, Virginia area during the Civil War. Nobody wanted to work there. Rumor had it that the building was haunted by the spirits of Union Soldiers who had died there, and some believed that the souls of Union dead were subjugated to the netherworld underneath the building itself—Hades.

The second of four parts of internship was surgery, which was divided into three one-month sections. One month of general surgery, one month of anesthesia, and one month of orthopedics.

General surgery consisted of watching, occasionally assisting, trying to learn which instrument to use for what. Standing next to the table in the OR, holding retractors, stretching a patient's muscles and skin to keep a surgical site open. Hour after hour, day after day. The surgeons rotated. The interns didn't. Interns stood for hours upon hours in their assigned operating rooms attending the surgeons. And there were eleven operating rooms. You were always on duty.

After weeks of standing in the OR with no breaks, Bill developed deep vein thrombosis, missed the entire month of anesthesiology, and was relegated to hospital treatment for four weeks. Which extended his internship from twelve months to thirteen. However, missing anesthesiology had one side effect that turned out to be to his advantage.

When the rest of the interns finished their tour after twelve months, Bill had to make up the month in anesthesiology that he had missed and got to spend his last month working alongside residents and assisting board-certified physicians. He was the only intern remaining. The other interns had finished and were gone.

"It was wonderful," Bill said. "I got hands-on participation in almost every procedure. I didn't have to share time with any of the other interns. Residents and attending physicians gave me all of their attention."

"A year later," Bill said, "When the Navy assigned me to a position on a carrier where I had to be qualified in anesthetics, I was very grateful for the special training those skilled experts in anesthesiology had given me."

Internal medicine consisted primarily of diagnostics and treatment. Interns were paired with a resident specializing in the field, and accompanied by the attending physicians—doctors already board certified in the field. Listening to hearts and lungs. Checking x-rays and diagnostic tests. Comparing symptoms with known diseases and chronic conditions. Putting a medical puzzle together and trying to come up with what was wrong, and what the treatment should be.

Hopefully without killing the patient.

Chapter 25
War Wounded

But by far, the most emotionally difficult of the three months in surgical training was the month in orthopedics. War was raging in Vietnam, and the wounded were triaged on site in the war zone in Nam into three classes of injuries.

Category one: "We can fix this injury locally and get the wounded man back into combat within a month."

Get-them-back-into-combat being the operative words.

Category two: "This wounded soldier is going to take a little longer before he can be sent back into combat."

That category of injured was flown to the Philippines and the medical work or rehab they needed was done there. After they were patched up, they were shipped back to Nam to finish their tour in combat.

Category three: "This injured person is never coming back. Load them up and ship them out."

Those soldiers had injuries that were life-threatening. They had critical or fatal wounds that would necessitate a surgical, burn, amputation, or trauma repair team beyond what triage or doctors in Nam or the Philippines could do. One destination for that category was Andrews Air Force base near Washington D.C.

Before they were transported from Vietnam, their wounds were patched on-site with a wet dressing and pinched shut with temporary sutures. Once they were somewhat stabilized, they were loaded on a C-130 and shipped to Andrews. When the C-130 landed, many were DOA. They didn't survive the flight.

And for most of those critical cases, it was just a matter of where they died. In Nam, on a C-130 headed home, or after they landed in the United States.

Medics and corpsmen on the C-130 transports fought for the wounded every moment of the trip home, trying to keep them alive, fighting to get them to a place where they could receive the kind of specialized emergency treatment they needed. But many of the injured were beyond hope, headed for help they would never reach in time.

For those who survived and made it as far as Andrews Air Force base, helicopters stood by to transfer them to military hospitals that were close to their own hometowns—so they could be near their families. Those who didn't make it during transport from Vietnam to the states—were processed at Andrews for burial, and their families notified.

Portsmouth was one of the specialized hospitals where the wounded were sent after their arrival at Andrews. Bill and other interns met the helicopters on the concrete in the Portsmouth hospital parking lot—where the helicopter medics and corpsmen transferred the injured. The interns moved those who hadn't survived the trip to Portsmouth to the morgue, evaluated and triaged those who were still alive for surgery, and gave assistance to those who needed immediate attention.

"Grab another stretcher," someone yelled. "Stuff something in that wound to stop the bleeding," a medic on the helicopter screamed as he handed a patient over to an intern. "Wound just broke open when I picked him up," he yelled. Every intern was involved in the transfer of the wounded. "Take this one to surgery first; I'm right behind you with one more. Well, no, too late. This one goes to the morgue."

It was pure chaos.

Many of the wounded were still in their military gear and uniforms. Most were covered in mud. Others were still hanging tight onto their rifles—arriving at the hospital straight from the fields of combat. In shock.

Learning how to be a doctor in wartime conditions was a trial by fire. You did things no doctor in peacetime would ever do, or would ever see. You were constantly applying everything you knew, and everything you had learned to do—to try and keep someone alive for a few more minutes. Sometimes succeeding. Sometimes not.

By the time the month was up, Bill had encountered and dealt with more horrendous and critical injuries than a civilian doctor would see in their entire lifetime. Death and dying were now his common enemies. Tragedy came with every helicopter that landed and opened its doors at Portsmouth.

Chapter 26
Avoiding War

Having learned the truth concerning the unfavorable survival rate and horrible conditions of his future as a Navy doctor in the killing fields of Vietnam, Bill poured his heart and mind into achieving the only possible way to escape that fatal assignment. He had to get into flight school after his internship was finished. His tour as an intern at Portsmouth hospital, unloading and treating dead and wounded coming in from Vietnam on med-evac helicopters, had exposed him to the ravages of a war that he never wanted to see any part of again—with its useless waste of human life.

And even if he was accepted into flight school, even if he could actually get in, he had to pass everything that all of the other non-medical flight cadets passed before he could go to flight surgery school at the Naval Aerospace Medical Institute—NAMI.

And even if he got there, he had to rank in the top four of a class of fifty-seven—no easy task. Flight surgery school only had four billets that weren't assigned to Viet Nam. Two of them, San Diego and the Naval Air Station Oceana at Virginia Beach were favorites. The other two were Adak Alaska—out on the tip of the Aleutian Islands where it stayed snow-locked, and Keflavik, Iceland, where nobody wanted to go. Everyone else was going to a Marine helicopter squadron. All but the top four graduates were going to war.

In a letter to Janet that week he wrote, "I have to get into flight school or I'm going to Vietnam. If I can get in, pass flight school, go to aviation surgery school, and rank at the top of that, there are four billets that don't have to go to war. One billet is in Alaska and one in Iceland—which aren't much better than the war. But first, I have to get into flight school."

"You're not even through with your internship!" she wrote.

"Yeah, but I'm trying to look ahead and figure out what I need to do next. Talking about next, when are you coming home?"

"I check out next week. I'm going to Europe for a month; my folks are joining me there. Dad was raised in Wales and wants to go back and visit."

"If you come through Europe, that means you'll be landing on the east coast instead of San Francisco when you enter the USA. What's the chance of you stopping in Portsmouth? They don't give us any free time off, but if I know ahead, maybe I could trade duty with one of the other interns."

"I could possibly do that—stop at Portsmouth. I'll let you know."

He was ecstatic. She didn't say no. Now all he had to do was find someone who was willing to take an extra shift for a couple of days. Actually, that wasn't possible. A couple of days were out of the question. A couple of hours was the most he could hope for. Every intern was already working a hundred hours a week. Sometimes more. Fourteen-hour days were standard.

Their schedules were insane, but he had made one friend who might help him. Jim McBee had begged Bill to cover for him once. He said that if the supervisor started looking for him, to tell the supervisor that he had gone to the bathroom. Bill agreed; Jim turned his pager off and locked himself in a broom closet to sleep. It wasn't unusual to be given a double shift. Forty-eight hours in a row. All the interns stayed dead on their feet.

Sleep was a rare commodity. Bill had snapped awake more than once sitting at a desk filling out paperwork. Coming to, slumped over the desk, pen in his hand, without even knowing that he had fallen asleep—until his pager went off. Waking up and wondering why he had a pen in his hand.

Chapter 27
The Answer

She wrote, "I'll stop. Find me a place to stay."

"I have a two-bed apartment. You'll have a room if that's acceptable to you. Talk to your folks. See if it's OK with them. I'm honorable. You're honorable. I promise I won't make a pass at you. I'm too tired to make a pass at anyone anyway. I have a couple of married friends you could stay with, but you'd have to sleep on their couch.

"I don't have a dime to my name or I would find you a hotel. But if I did that, I'm afraid I wouldn't see you at all because I work every day from six in the morning to ten at night—with overtime most days. Up to a hundred hours a week—seven days a week. You would have to take me to work if you wanted the car."

"Give me your address, tell me where the key to your apartment will be. I'll rent a car, pick up something and fix dinner. I don't know which day I'll be there yet. I'll let you know."

"You don't need to rent a car. The airport is fifteen minutes from the hospital. I can slip out for that. Someone will take my pager and cover me for an airport run. You can bring me back here, keep the car, then pick me up at ten.

"You'll cook!" Bill sounded excited. "I've forgotten what hot food tastes like. I've been existing on baby food. They stock jars in a closet in the pediatric ward. If it wasn't for that, all the interns would starve. It's amazing what you will eat when you are hungry with no choices. More often than not, we dip our fingers in the jars because we don't have a spoon. I think we're turning into animals. I've almost forgotten how to use a fork."

"You want to try chopsticks?"

"No thanks. I'll use my fingers—I have practice."

"You aren't going to use your fingers! Surely, you have silverware."

"Somewhere. When you look in the cabinets, you'll find pots and pans and silver that I've never used. Sleep has become more critical than food."

She gave him a date for her return, and when she landed, Bill gave his pager to his friend McBee and drove to the airport.

She was beautiful. He had almost forgotten how pretty she was.

"Hi," he said. He was pretty well tongue-tied. What do you say to someone you haven't seen in two years and want to impress? "I can't tell you how happy I am you decided to do this. You look great; China seems to have agreed with you."

"And you look terrible," she said. "You have dark circles under your eyes and you've lost weight. Eating baby food and not getting any sleep doesn't seem to agree with you."

"I know. I'm pretty well whipped. I'm ready for home cooking. I wish I could spend the afternoon with you, but I have to go back to work. You can take the car if you'll pick me up tonight at ten."

"I can do that. We'll talk later."

"You may have to yell to make sure I'm awake. Sometimes I can't even tell when I'm asleep. I've learned to sleep standing up with my eyes open."

She stopped at a grocery store then followed directions to his apartment. She had traveled light. Most of her things had already been shipped to Oklahoma.

After she deposited her suitcase in the spare bedroom, she sat down in his living room and asked herself, "What am I doing here?"

It wasn't the first time she had asked herself that question.

The answer was simple. "I need to know."

She drove to the hospital at ten. He crawled into the passenger seat, said hello, and immediately fell asleep. He was quietly snoring by the time she pulled into his driveway.

"Wake up sleepy-head," she whispered. "You need food; I left dinner on warm."

Bill shook his head, figured out where he was, who was driving his car, then reached across the seat and squeezed her arm. "I'm sorry. Not a very warm welcome. Good thing you're driving; I would have fallen asleep at the wheel."

"Let's get hot food down you."

"Lead me to it." He ate and ate. And ate.

"You're going to make yourself sick!"

"It's worth it. I can't begin to tell you how good this is. I haven't had anything like this in months. Maybe years."

They exchanged small talk about what they had been doing for the last two years before he began to nod off again.

"I'm sorry again," he apologized. "I'm dead on my feet; I can't stay awake. Take me into work at six in the morning and I'll see if I can't trade a couple of hours off with Mac, or someone else, and you can pick me up in the evening at eight."

"I'll have breakfast for you at five-thirty in the morning and make you a sandwich for lunch. I'm going to go shopping while you're at work. I want to buy some new clothes. I need some American Levi's that are made for women who are taller than five feet."

The next night, she picked him up at eight, and they sat down in his kitchen to eat the meal she had cooked. He reached across the table and held her hand. "I'm really glad you came."

She squeezed his fingers and said, "I am too."

Every moment he was free during that week, they talked; they caught up on their lives. And finally, the day before she was leaving for Oklahoma, he told her, "I've asked you twice before to marry me. I'm asking you again. This is my third time. If you say no to me this time, I'm not going to risk rejection to ask you again. So—Janet, will you please marry me?"

"I will."

"You will?!"

"Yes."

He was dumbfounded.

"But there is a problem," she added. "You have to get yourself back on the right side of God."

He was more than ready to find his way back to God. It was like a weight had been lifted from his soul.

Chapter 28
Going AWOL

He took her to the airport the next day, kissed her goodbye at the gate, and asked her, "When?"

"Soon," she said. "Before I back out."

"I love you," he said. "Don't back out, I don't think I could stand waiting another eight years for you to decide to date me again—much less marry me. Call me," he continued. "Let me know when. It's going to take some doing on this end to get away from here."

"Calling you won't work. You are so busy that I'd never be able to get through to you. You call me—during the day sometime when you can. When your pager isn't buzzing. And—I love you, too."

It was almost unbelievable. She was going to marry him. She loved him, too.

He went back to the grind. Trying to figure out how he was going to get away from Portsmouth, how he was going escape the hospital to go to Oklahoma and get married. There wasn't any legal way to do it. He would have to go AWOL. And that would necessitate a plan.

"Mac, I have a problem," Bill shared with his friend.

"So do we all, buddy. So do we all. It's called sleep deprivation."

"No, this one involves breaking the law and I need somebody to help me do it. I need four or five somebodies to help me do it."

"You're serious?"

"Dead serious."

"Shoot! Sounds like fun! What's going on?"

"She said yes. And I got a date. September 19. In Oklahoma."

"And just how do you plan to pull that off?" Mac asked him. "The Navy won't give you leave. They don't give us time off for anything for that matter. Ever."

"I think I could fly there on Friday night, get married on Saturday, and be back here that night or the next day. But that's where I need some help. I'd have to have every one of you cover for me. I'd have to leave my pager with you guys and you'd have to pass it around when I'm supposed to be on duty."

"It would look like I was making rounds and there's an outside chance nobody would find out. If someone came looking for me, you could use the same excuse we use when you're asleep in the broom closet. Tell them I'm in the bathroom. I'd pay all of you back with time and a half in return for covering for me—when I get back."

"This is crazy. But let me talk to the others—I'll see what we can do. As for time and a half, that's not possible. If you add half hours to what all of us are already doing, there aren't that many hours in a week."

"OK, but I'll do whatever it takes if you'll help me."

Chapter 29
Cold Feet

"I've made a mistake; I'm not sure how I can do this," Bill told Janet. "I don't know what I was thinking. I don't have time to be a married man. Even if I can pull it off to get there, I'm going to owe my buds here time and a half when I get back. I wouldn't be able to see you for at least a month after the wedding because I'd be working my shift and some of theirs."

"I've reserved the church, bought a dress, ordered the flowers, and called my minister from Kansas University to come to Oklahoma and marry us. What is wrong with you! You've been trying to get me to marry you for eight years!"

"I'm going to have to break the law to get to Oklahoma," he told her. "I could lose my internship. I could lose any hope I have to take my boards for National certification."

"On the other hand," she told him, "You could lose me."

There was silence on both ends of the phone until she said, "I actually do understand. I've got cold feet too. Wait a week and call me back. I've been praying really hard about this; I told God that if this isn't his will, to let me catch the measles on the nineteenth so I won't be able to show up for the wedding. I've never had the measles."

One week later, he called her, "I'm sure. I just got scared. This is forever and it overwhelmed me."

"If I have the measles when you get here, you can turn around and fly back to Portsmouth with my blessing."

Two people with doubts equaled four cold feet. But on the nineteenth of September, her pastor from Kansas University stood at the altar and pronounced the beautiful bride and the AWOL Navy medical intern, man and wife. God had decided. She didn't get the measles—and he didn't get caught by the military police going AWOL.

When the cake had been cut and punch served, guests threw rice and wished the newlyweds happiness—giving them a royal send off for their honeymoon.

There was no honeymoon. Bill had to show up at work the next day or he would be arrested. They spent the night in Tulsa, then caught an early morning plane to Portsmouth.

For two people who had struggled eight years to get to the alter, fate was about to give them a second chance to back out of the deal if there were any doubts about their decision.

That evening, when Bill got home from work, the phone rang. It was their home town preacher Frosty Jackson. "I've got some really bad news," he told them. He sounded completely shook up. "The Kansas preacher that performed your marriage ceremony didn't have a legal license to marry someone in Oklahoma. Your wedding ceremony wasn't valid. I'm really sorry to have to tell you this."

"You've got to be kidding," Bill said.

"What do you mean? Are you saying that we weren't actually married after all!" Janet had a hard time getting the words out.

"No, I'm telling you the truth. One of the guests at your wedding, a lawyer, was joking with the Kansas preacher and said it was a good thing that he had an Oklahoma license. The Kansas preacher replied that his license was good everywhere in America. Imagine his surprise when he learned that it wasn't any good in Oklahoma. You have to have an Oklahoma license to preform a ceremony here. So, what I'm telling you is that the ceremony wasn't legal. You two weren't married."

Bill looked at Janet and took her hand. "Do you want to be my wife?" he asked her. "Will you marry me again?"

"Yes, I do. And I will. Do you want to be my husband?"

"I do."

"Well," Frosty answered. "I actually have good news. After the two of you left, I stepped in to save the day. All you actually needed to get married in Oklahoma was a legal minister's signature. So, while all of your guests watched, I took a pen—waved it in the air with great flourish, spread the license out on a nearby table and signed it. When the ink was dry, I held it up to heaven, cleared my throat and announced to the crowd, "I now pronounce them man and wife. You didn't even have to be here! The reception crowd roared their approval as they witnessed your second marriage ceremony," Frosty told them."

"Actually, the important thing is that I've saved you both from living your lives in sin."

Chapter 30
The Intern

Within days after they returned to Portsmouth, Bill was notified that he had been accepted to flight school—which would have been a dead dream if he had been caught going AWOL to Oklahoma to get married.

Even though they were legally married, it was months before they actually had an entire day together. To fill the hours when she was left alone, Janet painted and took a class in photography. Bill picked up his schedule once again—a schedule that continued to be unrelenting even though his friends let him off the hook and didn't extract the time and a half. They all gave him a few hours apiece as a wedding present.

It was not a very normal marriage—but neither of their lives had been what the world would consider normal up to that time anyway. They made it work because they were both committed. To each other, to the institution of marriage, and to God himself.

It was the following July when he finally made up the month he had missed in anesthesiology and had taken his national boards. State boards followed, which gave him a license in the state of Virginia to practice medicine—and certified him in a number of other states as well. He was now officially qualified as a physician. His internship was done. Free at last, free at last; Thank God Almighty—free at last.

But the Navy was not done with him. He had three more months to do. They assigned him as the duty officer in charge of the Portsmouth emergency room for the rest of the summer, and every day was a new adventure in the ER. You never knew what was coming in.

Late on a Friday night, the ambulance brought in three guys that had the crap beaten out of them. The military kept an ambulance parked in front of

Harry's White Horse Tavern on Friday nights because that was payday, and there was always a fight and somebody needing stitches.

Bill sewed all three of them up, then asked what happened. "Killer did it," one of them replied. "He like'ta killed me."

"Where were you when this happened?" All four of them gave Bill the same answer, including a Marine sergeant who was so big he looked like a sumo wrestler.

"I was at this bar, minding my own business, and this wild karate, kung-foo guy tore into me and beat the snot out of me."

About that time, a second ambulance arrived and unloaded a tiny Asian man.

"It's him!" the Marine yelled. "It's Killer! Keep him away from us."

Bill ended up putting stitches in the head of a tiny shrimp of a guy called Killer who had a black belt in karate. The Marines who had been whipped didn't want to lose face by telling Bill they had been clobbered by someone half their size.

A small Air Force base in the area had its share of casualties as well. Three Air Force MPs in full uniform rolled a gurney through the emergency room door with a fourth MP lying on it who had his chest, knees, and wrists strapped to the gurney.

"What's the deal?" Bill asked them.

"He went nuts. Completely bonkers. He was in the guard house—he pulled out a forty-five and started yelling and shooting. It took all three of us to contain him and get him here."

Bill checked the MP who was strapped down, and remarked, "He seems calm."

"He may look that way, but you need to be careful; with his training, he's dangerous. He's really strong; he could kill you with his bare hands."

Bill asked the patient, "Are you going to cooperate and be calm if I unstrap you to examine you?"

The strapped-down MP nodded his head. "Yes, sir," he replied.

Bill removed the straps and the instant the straps were undone the man jumped up off the gurney and went crazy, tearing at the other guys, biting and scratching. The three MPs shoved him into an exam room and locked the door.

"Told you so, doc."

Bill called Mental Health and thought to himself, "I should have learned my lesson when the nurse unstrapped the guy trying to catch the train to Poteau."

When the constantly crazy three months in the ER were finished, he and Janet headed to Pensacola, and Bill checked into flight school.

His schedule seemed like a vacation. He only had to work from six to five. And for the first time since they were married, he had time for his wife. They ate breakfast together each morning, and dinner each evening. It was like the honeymoon they had never had.

He didn't tell her that he was scared to death every morning when he got in a plane. Flying wouldn't ever be his real job—but he had to go to classes and pass twelve checks just like every other flight cadet. The difference was that he was scared spitless all the time. He had never wanted to be a pilot—it was just a means to an end. He had to qualify to fly to become flight surgeon. And even then, he had to graduate at the top of his class to be able to stay stateside and not go to war. He had his doubts as to the sanity of his plan—because it meant that he had to solo to qualify.

After eleven flight checks were finally completed, he couldn't get out of it—he had to do the twelfth. He had to get in an airplane all by himself and solo. He certainly didn't feel ready, much less qualified, but he crawled into the cockpit, revved the engine, and prayed that spending the last seven years of his life becoming a doctor hadn't been wasted. Prayed that he wouldn't kill himself.

His last thought as his wheels left the runway was something his Marine jet jockey brother-in-law Ken had once told him, "You're going to die when it's your time to die. Every time I lifted off the runway for a combat mission, I was headed into fire. I figured I was a dead man already—and forgot about it. If you think about it, you can't do your job."

Bill somewhat successfully flew solo and got his wings—with an acorn for medicine on his wings instead of an anchor like the rest of the Navy pilots earned. He almost killed himself only twice. Once, when he got distracted by things happening on the ground, and barely missed a radio tower.

The second incident occurred when he was making the turn to land. Another plane was coming at him head-on. He swerved right, as did the other plane and they missed each other by inches. So close that he counted the rivets on the other plane's underbelly. Once he was on the ground, he thanked God he had survived and that flight school was behind him. The first part of his plan to escape being sent to Vietnam was over and done with.

He transferred to NAMI and began the aviation studies to become a flight surgeon, learning all about the psychology of the aviator. What drives him, how to tell when he's on the edge, when he is sick and won't tell you for fear you will ground him. How to recognize that he is a danger to himself and others and he needs to be grounded—temporarily or permanently. Once again, the psychiatry classes he had been forced to take in Med school came to his rescue.

He worked his butt off to rank in the top four of the aviation flight class so that wouldn't be sent to war. He finished number three, which was his ticket to where he was going to be assigned. Number one and two would be stateside. Number three and four were going to Iceland or Alaska. But number two wanted to go to Nam, so Bill was elevated to a stateside billet. God in his mercy had looked down on him with grace. He wasn't going to war. He had already done his time with Vietnam's medevac helicopters, treating mortally and critically wounded combat troops. Fighting death. One horribly wounded soldier after another, and another, and another. Day, after day, after day.

The crazy number two classmate in flight school didn't want a stateside assignment. He wanted to be Kojac; he wanted to go to war and hang out the open waist gunner door of a helicopter and fire a machine gun—which was illegal for medics. Everyone in the class at NAMI thought the guy was nuts. Later, they heard that the wanna-be Kojac talked his way onto a helicopter, heisted a machine gun off a dead corporal, and never told anyone he was a medic. And re-upped for another year.

The rest of the flight surgeons just wanted their year in the Vietnam war to be over with—and live through it.

What Bill cared about was that he had a stateside billet—which probably saved his life. Out of fifty-seven billets, fifty-three doctors were immediately assigned to Marine helicopter units in Vietnam. An assignment where doctors continually were trying to keep the wounded alive while staying alive themselves. Many of his classmates didn't return. Viet Cong snipers targeted medics and physicians in order to destroy the American troops' morale—identifying them by the red cross on their sleeves and executing them by putting a bullet through their helmets.

News feed: The Hospital Corps is the most decorated rating in the Navy. Navy corpsmen have earned:
22 Medals of Honor,
179 Navy Crosses,
959 Silver Stars.
More than 1600 Bronze Stars
And 20 ships have been named in honor of corpsmen.

The highest percentage of sniper fatalities of any unit was medics. The first target a Cong sniper would try and eliminate was a medic. And they were very good at it.

Chapter 31
Two More Years

Years before, in 1940, when war was looming on the European front, naval aviators were pressed to find auxiliary landing strips on which to train. The government paid a paltry thirty-five thousand dollars for three hundred and twenty-eight acres in Virginia, and the Navy built a small airfield and dive-bombing site. By the time it was officially commissioned as the Naval Auxiliary Air Station Oceana, in August of 1943, it had to rapidly be expanded to meet the demand for trained fighter pilots headed to the war in Europe.

Oceana was seen as the 'tip of the spear' by the Navy Department, and in 1951 an additional 3800 acres were added with dual eight-thousand-foot runways, 260,000 square yards of aircraft parking, and storage for two-hundred and fifteen million gallons of jet fuel. Which provided a permanent base for four carrier air groups.

Norfolk, Virginia was at the center of a sprawling complex of towns including Oceana. Bill and Janet arrived in 1972 after the base had been dramatically expanded. Five of the six Atlantic Fleet carrier air wings with multiple squadrons were based there—as well a squadron of Marines. It had evolved into an enormous base where the Navy trained pilots on airfields as well as on carriers operating ten miles off-shore.

It took a week to get checked in, find housing, and get moved into a house on a bayou, an inlet off Chesapeake Bay with a pier. It was heaven on earth.

It was apparent Oceana was about ships and airplanes. Not medicine. Bill's role was going to be lending medical support for a military machine that had arms like an octopus stretching out over thousands of acres.

Some days he worked at the base clinic, taking care of the general health of families on base. Runny noses, strep throat, flu, routine health problems. No major challenges. Compared to the practice of medicine at Portsmouth, this was a piece of cake. Lots and lots of children; most adult patients he saw were under forty-five. Older people who had medical problems associated with aging were few, limited to those retirees in the area.

Chapter 32
Pilots

Most days Bill taught medical classes for pilots. Classes that prepared them to recognize physical signs that they were in trouble—before they climbed into a cockpit. Which included a long list of items. They needed to know how to safely eject from an airplane and the problems associated with surviving in water, ice, snow, or the jungle to name a few.

Additionally, there were dozens of 'trouble' signs a pilot needed to be able to recognize once they were in the air. Not that what Bill had to say meant that much to a pilot one way or another; pilots didn't want to listen to anyone's advice—including a doctor. Jet jocks believed they were invincible—until they had a serious emergency. Then they became more reasonable and would sometimes listen.

Each squadron had its own flight surgeon responsible for qualifying a pilot fit to fly. Pilots lied, covered up physical conditions that would get them grounded, and generally did everything else they could do to stay in the air. Which created an uneasy relationship between the flight surgeon and the pilot. If the FS said you were unfit to fly, you were grounded. Unless the squadron commander said the flight was critical. Pilot safety was always secondary to the mission.

The flight surgeon got to know each pilot in his squadron well—because he flew with them on a regular basis to evaluate their performance in the air. Were they nervous? Were they distracted, showing signs of distress such as repeated swallowing, sweating, making repetitive motions of fingers, hands, stretching their neck, or shifting around in their seat as they got ready to take a catapult shot?

He flew with them for their cat shots, hook landings, and overall flight checks. He had to fly as many hours as they did. But the assignment as to who the flight surgeon would fly with on any given day was random so that the pilot never knew who it was going to be, or when the flight check would happen. Pilots were always trying to out-think and outwit the flight surgeon. The classes he had taken at NAMI in aviation psychiatry once again proved to be invaluable.

A normal person would go see a doctor when something was wrong. Not a fighter pilot. When a pilot was forced to get checked by the flight surgeon, he was doing just the opposite. Trying to convince the doctor that absolutely nothing was wrong with him.

One pilot memorized the eye chart. After he got in his plane, he would put on his thick coke-bottom eyeglasses so that he could see.

Another flew with a bleeding ulcer for weeks before he finally passed out. Luckily, he was on the ground, and was sent to surgery to remove half of his stomach.

Another went bankrupt; he couldn't make ends meet and became unstable. His solution was to bail out of his plane over water, swim to shore, and vanish so that his wife could declare him dead and collect his insurance.

The classes he took at NAMI to understand the personalities and thinking processes of military pilots were invaluable. It took the skill of a detective to figure out what was really going on in their heads. Sometimes you succeeded. Sometimes you didn't.

Pilots took the warnings about problems they might encounter while they were in the air more seriously—since there were only three ways to get out of an airplane. You could successfully land it, eject, or you could crash and burn. No pilot particularly wanted to crash and burn or eject. Ejections usually caused some sort of injury. Landing the airplane was by far the best method of getting out of the plane and a good landing was the one you walked away from.

Chapter 33
Flying Again

The A-6 was the top airplane in the Navy, a two-seater with the seats side by side; Bill flew second seat as the Bombardier navigator. Everything in the A-6 was computer controlled. His job was to fix vectors and altitude, tell the pilot where to turn, where to go, monitor fuel—do everything that needed to be done except fly the thing.

He was forced to take cat shots and carrier landings on a regular basis with some random pilot that he could only pray was physically and mentally fit to fly the airplane. You never knew for sure. He was scared to death every time he climbed into a plane on the carrier. He was all too familiar with what things looked like when something went wrong. Which they were prone to do.

Every time there was an accident, the accident board personnel changed—except for Bill and the Master Chief. As the accident board human resource expert, Bill was responsible for everything that had touched the pilot in a crash. Ejection seat, flight suit, gloves, survival gear. Which included both carrier and land accidents.

There was nothing in life as frightening as aviation carrier work. Bill prayed every day that he could finish his last two years in the Navy without ending up in a box in the ground at Arlington. Prayer compounded by the fact that every time they put a pilot in a box to ship him for burial, the flight surgeon had to be the one who dug him out of what was left of the plane and categorize every item. Helmet, boots, gloves, and body parts.

One pilot failed a landing, flipped sideways, and ejected into the wall of the tower. The navigator flying with him rotated over with the plane and ejected upside down into the carrier deck.

Another pilot boltered three times, failed to hook a wire, and was told to shunt to shore, but he had bingo fuel and couldn't make it. He had two choices, try a fourth time to hook wire or eject. He was terrified. Primary flight control in the tower told him to fly alongside the carrier and eject and they would pick him up.

Once he moved into position, everyone was primed, watching him, waiting for him to eject. But he didn't eject. After flying alongside the carrier for a lengthy amount of time, he picked up speed and altitude, came back around, and hooked at the very moment he ran out of gas. The plane dropped like a rock out of the air and onto the deck.

When the pilot climbed out of the cockpit, flight control instructed him to come up to the tower. He arrived, shaking all over, carrying the ejection seat handle in his hand. Flying alongside the carrier, he had tried to eject over and over again, but the ejection handle had repeatedly failed. Flying on fumes, he had no choice but to try and land once again. His adrenaline level was so extreme that he had pulled the ejection handle completely out of the seat. Which is impossible. But he did it.

Another pilot also encountered a faulty ejection seat. A bolt broke and the seat fired him accidentally. The plane was destroyed, but the pilot should have been OK. However, not only did the ejection seat fail, the parachute failed to automatically open as well. Still strapped into the seat, falling toward the ground, he reached up over his head, and desperately tried to pull the parachute bindings open.

In the accident report, the board asked him, "What was the first thing you remember seeing the instant you got the parachute open?"

"Green. I saw trees." He had finally managed to rip the parachute open only feet from the ground.

The examiner told him, "There aren't any trees in the area where you landed. Your parachute opened in a swamp of green reeds."

The pilot blanched when he realized how close he had come to being dead.

Later, parachute riggers in the warehouse tried to repeat what the pilot had done. They tried to disengage a parachute from an ejection seat, but none of them had the strength. They couldn't do it.

Bill explained, "Sometimes, there are things a person can do that are humanly impossible. When they are terrified and their body is jolted with adrenaline."

Catapult shots were the most feared thing a pilot had to learn to do. When you were shot off the carrier, you were supposed to veer very slightly to the left to get out of the path of next plane that was getting shot off behind you. One beginner veered too far, couldn't get enough lift, rolled, and ejected upside down into the water. There were a million ways to kill yourself in a jet plane—as well as kill your navigator. And Bill was the navigator for all of their test flights.

At Portsmouth, unloading critically wounded and the dead from Vietnam when the medivacs flew them in, had somewhat prepared him for the job. But those dead and wounded men had been anonymous. These dead pilots were personal. He knew them and they were in pieces. There were loved ones to notify.

Chapter 34
PTSD

By the end of a year, he had PTSD. He recognized the symptoms, made an appointment with the squadron commander, and turned in his wings. "I can't do this anymore," he told the commander. "I'm done."

With every dead pilot he had to extract, he pictured his brother-in-law Ken who operated off a carrier every day. It could have been him. He couldn't seem to get that out of his mind.

The old saying, "Physician heal thyself," seemed a reasonable course of action. He had the background in psychiatry to diagnose himself. But diagnosing and treatment are two entirely different animals. He really believed that he would be able to treat himself. Smart people are sometimes incredibly stupid.

His solution was to quit feeling. To bury his emotions. To diagnose and treat patients without getting too close to them. That way, if the patient couldn't be helped, if they were going to die, the pain would be bearable.

Sometimes he still became woozy at the sight of blood—it was never predictable. Blood could be gushing everywhere and he had no problem. Then someone would come in with a cut that would drip and he would lose it. He didn't know what triggered his reactions.

There were other problems that were serious—things that would give him difficulty. He could stitch up and repair any part of the body except hands. Wounded hands defeated him emotionally every time. He didn't know or understand why. Nurses who worked with him, those who knew him well, kept his secret; they stood on either side of him when he had to stitch fingers or palms—ready to catch him if he started to pass out. Other triggers were certain odors. Burning nylon, grilled pork, jet fuel.

The Navy sent him to a physiatrist specializing in PTSD for an evaluation. He quizzed Bill about what he thought caused his inability to operate on the palms or hands. Why did he faint?

"You've written a detailed report on every part of every accident you've worked. You've been exposed to the most horrific details imaginable over and over again. What do you think happens to cause the subsequent reaction when you deal with hands?"

"I don't know," Bill told him.

"I write a report on every accident in detail, but I have no memory of anything from any of those accidents concerning a pilot's hands. Obviously, I wrote those reports. But I don't remember anything I wrote about the gloves, whether they were still on or off, were they burned or not. Nothing about fingers, wedding rings—nothing. I wrote a report about every part of what was left of the pilot's body. I just don't remember anything about any of their hands."

Everyone in the profession admired his skills. Everyone in the profession considered him brilliant. He was. But on the inside, he was a wreck.

PTSD is a strange malady. It all happens inside your brain and presents itself at odd moments for unexplainable reasons. Every case is different. Bill learned over time to control it—bury it, and keep on keeping on. Few were aware of the demons that haunted him.

It would be many years before he got the help that he needed.

Chapter 35
Checking Out

The last year in the Navy, Bill helped civilian organizations and churches that were trying to address the problem of drugs and drug addiction in the Virginia Beach area—which at the time, had the highest illegal drug availability and purity in the U.S. It was a party town with a hippy culture. The Navy had its drug problems as well.

He assisted the Virginia Department of Human Services. He regularly debated health education and welfare issues on television and in churches. He had become well-known in the state as a public figure and speaker. Nobody in academia was doing drug rehab or intervention training in the U.S. at the time. It was a relatively unknown field of medicine.

Four months before he received his discharge papers from the Navy, he was offered a position as Chief of Behavioral Science at a new university that was being established: Eastern Virginia Medical University. They wanted his unique expertise. He accepted their offer and signed a contract that would place him in charge of teaching behavioral science, as well as supervising medical classes in the psychiatry department.

Within weeks, he realized that he might have made a mistake by signing the contract. One Sunday in church, a missionary from India spoke about the critical problems in Asia—about the desperate need for medical volunteers.

A small voice tugged at Bill. 'China'. His response was immediate. "No."

He had developed a dislike for China and everything Chinese on the day Janet had left to go there. And waiting for her to come back to America, hoping for her to say, 'Yes, she would marry him,' had only intensified his dislike for the country. He didn't even like Chinese food.

Three years of college, four years of Med school, a year of internship, four years in the active Navy—eight years in the Navy total. Finally, he was ready to do three years of residency. It had already been a grueling regimen to become a doctor—and it wasn't over yet. He didn't have time to think about missions. Especially in China.

His new job at the University would start in July when he got out of the Navy; however, he was unsettled. Why did he think about China that day in church? What did it mean? He had a signed contract with the University in Virginia, so why explore anything else. But one evening when they were eating dinner, Janet asked him, "What would you think about us going to China to the mission field someday? How would you feel about that?"

Even though they had not discussed it; she had been thinking about what the missionary had said that day in church as well, and she naturally had a heart for China. She had lived there for two years.

"I signed a contract," he told her, "Legally, it's a done deal. It would cost a lot of money that we don't have to get out of it—or an intervention from God himself. Otherwise, I'm going to be Chief of Medical studies in psychiatry at a new University in Virginia."

How would you get out of a legally binding contract; and did he even want out—to go to a place where he didn't want to go? But conviction nagged at him that going to China might be God's will for their lives.

The problem was that no missionaries had been allowed inside China since 1949. China had a ban on missionaries, preachers, journalists, and most foreigners unless they had a business reason to be there. You couldn't get into China just to wander around. Why would God present a conviction for him to go to a place where the doors were closed and you couldn't get in?

It was unsettling. Christianity comes with a bit of a problem. First, you have to want God's will for your life. And second, you have to be willing to do it. Giving Him your permission to work out whatever details he wants to work out is one thing. Letting him do it however he wants to do it is another. You have to let go of it.

In the middle of all those confusing thoughts, they went home to Pryor for Christmas. On Christmas Eve, an unexpected phone call came from the Dean of the Virginia University telling Bill that he needed to come back there immediately. The federal accreditation boards of Virginia had approved all of the multiple contracts that had been written by the University administration—contracts that had to be verified in order for the hospital to be built and staffed.

However, the board had objected to one paragraph in one contract. It was the contract that the university had made with Bill. The one he had signed. He had to come back to Virginia immediately and appear in person to sign the revised copy.

God had intervened.

"No," he told the dean. "I can't sign it. Thank you for your consideration, but you'll have to find someone else. I'm going to go to China as a missionary."

"What do you mean! That's not possible. They don't accept visitors. They don't let missionaries into China. You won't be able to get in!"

"I can, and I will," he told the dean.

Chapter 36
Undercover Agent

If you were writing a soap opera, the events of his life would already qualify. At this point, intervention by God didn't seem that unusual.

Once Bill was free of his contract with the university in Virginia, he and Janet immediately contacted the IMB—the International Mission Board for the Southern Baptist Convention, and volunteered to go to China. Baptists made the process easy. They paid for training, language school, housing, and salaries for their people, which meant that volunteers wouldn't have to spend time in the U.S. begging churches for funds to support them.

They were approved. But since the doors to China were closed, they accepted an appointment to the Philippines, with the hope that someday they could transfer.

The week before they were to leave, someone came banging on their front door.

"Thank God you haven't left yet." It was Charlie, an IMB missionary doctor in charge of the hospital in Mindanao—an island at the southernmost tip of the Philippines.

"I barely got out," he told them. "Some of the others didn't make it. I need to warn you about what's going on where they are sending you because the IMB is telling people that it's safe. It's not! The board in Manilla has gotten the wrong information and it's going to put people in danger."

"The Muslim Moros are killing Christians at the place where they are sending you. You need to contact the Mindanao hospital where I was in charge and get verification directly; talk to them. There is still an American and one other nurse there. The rest are Filipinos. You absolutely must not go there right now."

Charlie continued, anxiety in his voice, "One of our missionaries tried to find out what was going on down there, got a plane, and flew over the area. Call him if you need more information. The Moros shot him down. But he survived the crash; Filipino friends got him out. He was lucky. I felt like I had to warn you in person. Don't go. I'm telling you, don't do it."

After Charlie left, Bill called the hospital board in Mindanao; they verified the situation warning him that it was foolish and extremely dangerous for Christians to even think about coming to Mindanao until the Filipino government took control and stopped the Muslim Moros.

The IMB finally verified the information. It looked like he and Janet weren't going to the Philippines. The delay in leaving the states was providential; it probably saved their lives, but having finally made the decision to be a missionary doctor, Bill was totally frustrated by the events. This was not going to be their only delay; another one was coming, and this one would cost them two more years stateside. Janet had cancer.

Having finally returned to the faith in which he had been raised, having renewed his vows to God, and surrendered to the mission field, Bill didn't understand why this had happened to Janet. His questions were compounded by the fact that they had decided to start a family, and Janet was three months pregnant. Every time he prayed, his prayers started with, "Why?"

Surgery for the cancer was successful, but there was no way to know how the anesthetic during surgery had affected the baby. They waited. And in the middle of waiting, they received the news that due to the cancer diagnosis, the IMB had withdrawn approval for them to become missionaries. The board had regulations concerning funding for people with medical conditions. They would not be eligible again until 10 years post-surgery. Doors had slammed shut.

It's hard to know what to do next when your life is turned upside down, but one thing was certain—he had to have a job to support them. They had to eat. The immediate problem was solved when a doctor in their hometown invited him to come help in his clinic. Bill took the job since he was unable to predict what their future was going to be. But in all of the confusion of their lives, the most important thing had turned out right. Six months after surgery, they had a very normal, perfect son. And named him Morgan. Janet's maiden name.

Two years later, the IMB unexpectedly contacted them. There was an opening in Hong Kong for a doctor, and the mission board had decided to make an exception to International Mission Board policy. He and Janet would be allowed to go to Hong Kong, and their health insurance would be paid—except for medical expenses related to her surgery or reoccurrence of any problems connected to it.

It wasn't mainland China, but it was close. However, there was another requirement before they could leave. He had to take twelve hours of seminary credit in religious studies before they could serve overseas.

It seemed like it was just one more delay on top of all of the other delays. But he resigned himself to the requirement, packed up, and went to Fort Worth. Twelve hours of credit was such a paltry amount of schooling after the multiple classes he had already endured, that he audited twenty-four more hours on the side.

There was a clinic at the seminary, and the month after they arrived, the doctor who ran it died. The dean asked Bill to take the position and promised him a quick, 'good old boy' license for the state of Texas. Bill took the job, got the Texas license, then spent the entire semester refusing the dean's daily attempts to recruit him to stay at the seminary as the permanent clinic physician. China was his destination, not Texas.

Chapter 37
Hong Kong

In 1976, after multiple roadblocks and much frustration, Bill and Janet arrived in Hong Kong and began a two-year program in language school. They had to learn to speak Cantonese. It was an IMB requirement that missionaries know the language of the country where they were going to serve. They were given instructions not to do anything else during that time. No outside jobs, or church work. Misunderstandings, or Cantonese language foul-ups, were something that the International Mission Board wanted to avoid.

In the New Territory, an area north of the city that Hong Kong had just acquired, no Christian work was going on. Janet's familiarity with the multiple islands of Hong Kong made it easy for them to violate the strict rules and begin teaching a Bible class—which was the reason they had volunteered for missions in the first place. The Maverick had arrived. Some types of rules were made to be ignored.

By the time they had finished language school, things in mainland China had changed. Borders were opening up to the world's lucrative travel industry; however, China wanted to control what visitors saw and where they were allowed to go. The Chinese Travel Service devised a plan to permit certain select groups to enter—then assigned the visitors to handpicked, thoroughly trained guides.

Opening the country to visitors presented a problem. Trained Chinese travel guides had to be prepped ahead of time with pre-programmed answers for any questions the outsiders might ask.

In anticipation of this, the Chinese government asked the Hong Kong Chinese University if they could supply them with a trial group of visitors for the guides to practice on. The university could, and they did. Bill and Janet's

1977 language class was chosen to be the first official foreign group allowed to enter China since 1949.

There was only one road from Hong Kong into the mainland. It was reserved for trucks with merchandise, and was heavily guarded against unauthorized persons, including the group of language class members. Primed with excitement, the class members boarded the train headed to the only trestle that crossed the Lowu river between Hong Kong and mainland China.

Although the railroad trestle was the only point of entry, trains were not allowed to cross it. Hong Kong trains pulled up to the trestle, then unloaded their passengers and luggage.

Their group had been pre-approved to walk across the Lowu bridge and board a Chinese train on the other side. Janet became the first missionary to set foot in China in decades, with Bill one step behind her. They entered China's mainland and boarded the waiting Chinese train.

When it arrived at its destination, the train was met by the Director of Travel Service from Beijing—the top dog. He was there to observe this first interaction between visitors and the Chinese guides. The government's plan was to oversee training between the two groups. This question-and-answer portion between them was important and Beijing wanted to completely control it. All of it.

The director introduced himself, spoke to them in Cantonese, and told them to feel free to pose any and all questions they might have for the uninitiated guides.

When a question was posed that a guide didn't know how to answer, the director would switch languages from Cantonese to Mandarin to coach the guides, not realizing that he couldn't hide what he was saying, because the visitors spoke many different languages—not only Cantonese, but Mandarin, Japanese, German, and French among others. Someone would immediately translate what the director was saying and tell the group.

A Catholic priest, who had a Ph.D. in Chinese history—asked multiple questions about China's culture and history, as well as the conditions of the people who were living under the Communist government.

It was obvious that his questions bothered the director – who was observing that the guides he had appointed were becoming frustrated with the priest's questions. Guides were miserable for fear they would say the wrong thing.

In an effort to direct their attention elsewhere, the group was given a tour of lush farm fields—to show the effectiveness of the Communist system. But the group had already seen many farms as they rode the train from the Lowu bridge into China—farms that had no modern farm equipment. They had seen large numbers of workers bending over using primitive methods, digging into the dirt with their hands to hoe, plant, or harvest.

The director announced that in the old days, people used to pray to God for rain. But now, the Communist government used science. Since they had installed water pumps, prayer was unnecessary. Their system, Communism, was much better than democracy, emperors, or especially God—who was unreliable and was a myth anyway.

In addition, the director touted the superior medical attributes of acupuncture as a surgical method of pain relief, and offered them an opportunity to observe it being used as a bull was castrated—but they were hustled along and not given time to observe. Since China didn't have access to modern anesthetics, the director's lecture was nothing but hype.

It was an interesting introduction to the country Bill hoped to enter. He knew that forty years earlier, during the 1930s before the Communist takeover, there had been a Christian revival inside China—the largest revival in the history of the world. And many of those surviving Christians still lived there. There were also some Bibles still in existence that had been printed in Mandarin by the Christian Chinese Press.

The Communists permitted government-controlled token churches to continue to exist. However, they were not allowed to evangelize or go outside their own group to invite people in. There were strict criteria. Each church was assigned four or five leaders by the Communists. Leaders who reported on each other—and all of their lessons had to be pre-approved by the Public Security Bureau, the PSB—an entity akin to the CIA or the FBI.

Every group, business, organization, or entity in China had a member of the Public Security Bureau on their staff. Anything anyone said, or did, had to go through the PSB and be approved by them—which effectively killed open evangelism.

Chapter 38
A Medical License

Since their first day in Hong Kong, Bill had been attempting to get a medical license with no luck at all. There were only two ways to get one. You could graduate from Hong Kong's medical school, or acquire one through the British government—a government that had been less than helpful. The British had sovereignty in Hong Kong, and total authority over Hong Kong licensing.

However, the Portuguese in Macau were more accommodating. As long as you went through their political system. Macau belonged to China; however, there was an unwritten agreement between the Communists, the Portuguese, the Macau gambling syndicate, and the Triad societies—who were similar to the mob in America—as to who was in charge of what.

Those four entities controlled all of the business, gambling, entertainment, and prostitution in Macau. They determined how life inside the borders of the province would be run. Everyone knew which lines not to cross.

The border between Macau and China was lax—much more porous than the heavily guarded Hong Kong border. Although the IMB had no requests from Macau for a doctor, Bill was anxious to check the province out for himself.

It took an hour to cross the Pearl River delta waters before his boat docked. He was met by a missionary named Millie, who greeted him, efficiently commandeered him, and took him directly to the office of the Medical Director for the Portuguese government.

After a few minutes of chit-chat, the director asked Bill what his intentions were for visiting Macau.

"Well, sir, the truth is, I have a medical license in the USA, but I have had no luck at all in getting a license from the British to practice in Hong Kong; I thought perhaps I might have a chance of getting a license from the Portuguese. Here. In Macau."

The director replied, "You can't get a license in Hong Kong because you are dealing with the British. That's the way they are. They think they're really special stuff, when the fact is, they're just uptight and think they are royal. They are impossible to deal with. I can give you a medical license right this minute if you want to practice medicine in Macau."

The director opened a drawer in his desk, took out a paper form, filled it out, signed it, handed it to Bill, and said, "There's your license. Attach a picture and you are in business. To hell with the British."

Within the month, Bill learned that the Medical Director for the Portuguese government—who had issued him a license—had been fired. Portuguese approval for Bill to practice medicine had not gone through proper channels. The Portuguese government was very unhappy that the correct procedures had not been followed, and that a white, round-eyed American doctor now possessed a Portuguese Medical license without having received proper approval. They gave him two months to 'Get out of Dodge'.

But the horse was already out of the gate. Bill was officially a Macau medical doctor. Even though he had not been accepted by the Portuguese government, he had a piece of paper that said he was legal. The Chinese Communists and the Macau syndicate had yet to weigh in, but things looked hopeful. Macau, as well as every country in East Asia, desperately needed experienced doctors.

Millie helped the couple find an apartment and a reputable Amah for their son. They requested, and received, approval from the IMB to open a medical clinic in Macau—where Bill now had a medical license. He was in business.

Chapter 39
The Syndicate

Julie Fernandez had an extreme case of brittle diabetes—a rare, deadly form of the disease. As she traveled the world for her boss, she had trouble controlling her medical condition and properly taking her medications—it was very difficult to keep up with her prescription schedule with all of the time zone changes. She had gone to every doctor in Macau as well as doctors in other countries but had not received effective treatment. She was constantly sick. When she heard that an American doctor had opened a clinic in Macau, she immediately made an appointment.

Bill knew exactly how to treat her. He had spent a year of his residency under a world-class endocrinologist who had only accepted complicated diabetes cases. Bill had hands-on experience with rare diabetes conditions. He explained to Julie why her diabetes was not being controlled by the drugs and methods that she had been using.

Within weeks of putting her on a new regimen, she felt better than she had felt in her entire life, and was singing the praises of the new American doctor to anyone and everyone who would listen. Which turned out to be providential, because Julie, who was a good Catholic girl, was also the personal secretary for the head of the Syndicate, Stanley Ho. He trusted her with all of his international business transactions.

She opened doors for Bill to practice medicine that would have otherwise been shut, and introduced him to people he otherwise would never have met. She explained to her syndicate boss, Mr. Ho, that he needed to use the American doctor for his enterprise because the doctor spoke fluent Cantonese.

Stanley Ho controlled all shipping, hotels, casinos, and entertainment venues, along with horse races—horse races with trotters, carts, and jockeys. Racing was a huge sport in Macau, and Ho's jockeys constantly needed medical help for injuries incurred by mishaps on the track. They were regularly thrown out of carts and run over by a horse, or mangled by the cart's wheels. Mr. Ho needed an official doctor for his jockeys.

Mr. Ho also controlled The Crazy Paris Show. An entertainment review of Can-can dancers who performed in a show modeled on similar productions in Paris. Every hotel Stanley owned had some sort of entertainment, and he wanted to control all of the medical information concerning the people he hired. He needed an official doctor for the girls, the actors, and other staff—in addition to the jockeys.

The girls were white and French, and male Japanese tourists were enamored with them, spending huge amounts of money in Macau. To keep the money flowing, Ho made sure that the Japanese visitors were safe—even though the Chinese bitterly hated the Japanese. Japan had invaded China a few years before, and won a conflict against them.

But money was more important than old rivalries, and anyone who tried to mug or harm a Japanese tourist simply disappeared. That kind of thing was common; Macau was the wild west of Asia. A snake pit with no real law. Known worldwide as a hell-hole of debauchery. Off-limits for the American military. If there was ever a place that needed the gospel message, it was Macau.

A member of Ho's syndicated gambling organization approached Bill and explained that many of the doctors they had been using couldn't speak Cantonese. Would Bill consider taking the jobs for both the jockeys and entertainment personnel?

Bill accepted both jobs. The Portuguese might not have been happy with him, but the syndicate was very, very pleased. Bill now had his foot in the door to the medical community in Macau. The horse racing syndicate was especially ecstatic with their new doctor. Jockeys were hard to replace. Can-can girls, however, were a dime a dozen. Word spread that the American doctor would treat common people—not just the elite. Working both sides of the moral aisle opened the doors for him to reach the people. Using medicine as a vehicle to spread the word of God. Without getting arrested.

With acceptance came privileges and contacts. Free admission to all sorts of entertainment. Free hotels. Galas, car racing, dinners—anything that came along. Even though they seldom took advantage of the venue, he and Janet were always invited to be the guests of Sydney Ho. And occasionally they attended some of the more acceptable events. He was the official Christian doctor for people who needed the gospel the most.

Chapter 40
Opening Doors

The mission board's requirement that Bill learn Cantonese had proved to be critically important to getting his foot in the door of every echelon in Portuguese society. But it presented a problem to the doctors in Macau who only spoke Portuguese. They were losing their patients to the new doctor and were constantly complaining to the Portuguese government about the American doctor who spoke Cantonese and was stealing their business. It was one more reason for the Portuguese to throw him out.

The Chinese Communists on the other hand were elated. They had an American doctor who could speak the language and was certified to practice at Kiang Wu, the Chinese hospital in Macau.

When China began to open its doors—after having had no lines of communication with outside countries for decades, Bill presented a unique opportunity for the Chinese to have dialogue with the American medical community. This was invaluable. China needed modern medical equipment, as well as knowledge about new medical procedures being used in the outside world.

But the Chinese were proud and would never admit that they were second to any nation. Bill realized he would have to appear exceedingly humble to be able to convince the Chinese that China was bestowing a favor on the United States by allowing American doctors to observe China's medical facilities and practices. But first, he had to get inside the country. He needed a contact.

His contact literally washed up onto the Hong Kong shore. A Chinese doctor and two of his friends who were attempting to flee oppression inside of China, tried to swim across the China sea using ballooned pig bladders as floaters. The doctor's two friends didn't make it. They were eaten by sharks and died horrible deaths. But Dr. Shi reached the Hong Kong beach, fell on his face weeping, and cried out to a God he didn't know, "Your mercy has spared me. I will find you and serve you the for rest of my life."

As he searched for a place to learn about this God who had spared his life and helped him escape from China—he found a church and became a Christian. It was the Christian medical community that told him about a doctor in Macau who was trying to get into China.

When Bill and Dr. Shi connected, Bill had the contact he had prayed for. Shi wanted to go back into China and help his son get out. He needed the de facto international protection that traveling with an American doctor could give him. China wouldn't want an incident involving a citizen of the United States. Especially a doctor they were trying to recruit.

Shi knew the Communist director of the number one hospital in Guang Jou and was willing to schedule a meeting if Bill would stay with Shi every moment, and give him safety so that he wouldn't be arrested. It was a providential request, because years later Shi became complacent, went in by himself, was arrested, and died in a Communist concentration camp.

When Bill met the Guang Jou director, he asked if there was some way the director could intercede and effectuate an opportunity for American doctors to visit the Chinese hospital to 'learn about Chinese medical procedures'. He assured the director that America would be honored to have an opportunity to gain knowledge from the great country of China. He also assured him that the United States would be extremely appreciative if China would permit doctors to come there and observe.

In his mind, Bill was thinking, "The American Medical society has nothing to learn from you. I've been working in your hospital in Macau for over a year, and I've learned nothing. They are so far behind the United States that any medical information learned from a reciprocity agreement with America would be learned by the Chinese, and the only reason doctors would come here is because it would be a great vacation. People want to come because they're curious."

What he said out loud was, "In America, there is a deep desire on the part of our people to learn about the great, magnificent country of China. American doctors would be honored to have the opportunity to come here and would jump at the chance to learn what you have to teach them."

Bill once again thought to himself, "Your country is not even in the medical ball game. You have no anesthetics except acupuncture. Your medical knowledge is antiquated and obsolete. China has everything to gain, and nothing to offer."

But of course, he didn't say what he was thinking. He wasn't stupid. This director wanted to save face. Saving face was hugely important in China. And Bill was more than willing to give the director all of the faces he wanted as long as it opened a door for him to get into the country and begin establishing underground Christian missions.

"The Chinese medical community would be pleased to help teach your American doctors," the director replied. He then began to make a list of all of the medical equipment that he wanted America to send to them immediately—as a gift in repayment for China's generosity to accept their doctors.

"I will be glad to help implement that," Bill replied. "And as soon as I hear from the Americans, I will contact you."

Chapter 41
The Liaison

While working in the Macau hospital, Bill created an organization called Hospitals Without Walls. Since post-surgical patients inside the Macau hospital were dying at an alarming rate, Bill had started releasing patients from the hospital after they had surgery and sending them home to recover, with a nurse checking on them in their homes. The death rate of the patients who went home was dramatically lower than those who remained inside hospital care—and proved to be a far safer method for the patient.

When his program proved successful, he started training more community nurses to care for patients at home, something that had never been done before—anywhere. He cross-trained them to share the gospel and evangelize while caring for people who had never heard the story of Jesus.

Because Bill's medical concept of treating people in their homes had not been approved, two Hong Kong missionary surgeons—who had recommended Bill for his position in Hong Kong in the first place—stood up in an IMB board meeting and accused Bill of malpractice. Bill's nickname of 'The Macau Maverick' was well known at that point, and was probably accurate. Seeking approval for innovation didn't usually occur to him.

But the remarkable surgical survival rate Bill was having with patients in Macau by sending them home after surgery had been observed by the Hong Kong hospital board. Adoption of his methods had already begun for their own post-surgical patients with remarkable results.

The time was right—and this practice of sending patients home to recover soon became accepted worldwide. It was safer and it was much cheaper.

A number of years before, at a medical fellowship, Bill had met a Christian surgeon from Bowman Gray named Tim and they had become instant friends. Bill presented him with a unique proposal.

"I'm the only person in East Asia who has the contacts and connections to get doctors into China. Are you interested? I need an entire team and I thought you might want in on it?"

"Of course I'm interested!" Tim replied. "Let me get Bowman Gray on board and I'll get back to you."

Bowman Gray jumped at the opportunity to become the first American Hospital to have a medical exchange between China and the United States. Every doctor on staff wanted to be first in line for this unique opportunity.

"However, there is a problem for me to able to implement this," Bill told them. "I need to go on staff at Bowman as your Asian consultant. I have to have a title and credentials to negotiate between Macau as a subsidiary of the Communists, the Chinese, and any other Asian country that might want to take advantage of this same opportunity. I'm hesitant to get involved with something that I can't control on this end."

"I need official Bowman Gray credentials and some freedom to negotiate. But up front, it's only fair that you understand that my interest is not entirely medical; I'll be using medicine to get inside China and find ways to spread the Christian gospel. I need to be clear about my intentions to do that. Any doctors that come should probably be Christians and agree to Bible study and prayer each day as we go in. We need God in on this."

Tim wanted on board as a Christian, and Bowman accepted the medical end of the deal. Bill was hired as the Bowman Gray medical liaison to China and all of East Asia.

He immediately began to make connections inside Chinese Hospitals as he tried to determine where to place American doctors so that they could be most effective. Once that was done, Tim recruited specific specialties to go in. Optometrists, dentists, surgeons, and cardiologists. Bill was subsequently put on the board of CMDA—Christian Medical Dental Association—as their missionary consultant.

The first group that came were almost all Christians, but by the time they left to go home, one of the doctors who wasn't a believer was so impressed with the character of the mission work Bill was leading, that he accepted Christ. "I need something better in my life," he said. "And I think, I have found it."

Bill shared what happened with Tim, "Maybe I was wrong about you recruiting only Christians. Maybe there might be a double purpose in this?"

Chapter 42
Medical Equipment

After the first group of doctors was successful, the Chinese asked Bill to bring more doctors in—with more new medical equipment. Bill wrote Tim, I need specific medical equipment. And I need you to get it free. I've attached a list of what I need. See if you can make that happen.

Maybe the American government would fund it to just get their foot inside China—once they find out I'm already in and approved by the Communists. Maybe manufacturers might see it as an opportunity to do business in China—give the Chinese what they want for free at first, and once they use it, they'll want to buy more.

See what you can get—then transport it to Hong Kong immediately so I can get it shipped inland to the hospital at Guang Jou. That's where your next group of doctors will be working with the Chinese. They can demonstrate equipment and explain procedures when they arrive.

The Chinese don't even have ultrasound. Or any knowledge of inhalation anesthesia, endoscopy—you name it, they don't have it. And they won't know how to use any of the equipment. Prep the next group of doctors who are coming and tell them that they will have to set everything up themselves before they can teach doctors how to use the equipment.

"Got it," Tim replied.

The medical equipment Bill requested arrived just before the second group of doctors did. Guang Jou's Communist director tried not to look grateful, but it was apparent that he was excited.

China provided hotel rooms for all the medical team members in Guang Jou, along with a dinner in their honor. But the first morning after they arrived, there was an abrupt knock on Bill's hotel door as he was preparing to leave for the hospital. The Public Security Bureau's representative assigned to the

Guang Jou Chinese hospital pushed himself in, followed by seven other security personnel. Since every business, organization, committee, or any other entity had a member of the PSB assigned to them, there was no exception for the hospital.

"What is your group doing here?" The security force leader asked. "Are you missionaries?"

Eight men grilled Bill for over two hours.

"No," Bill replied. "We're doctors. We have approval from the Communist government to be here to work in your hospital."

Over and over again the security force asked Bill the same questions. Over and over again, Bill gave the same answers. Finally, when the leader of the PSB seemed satisfied with his answers, they turned to leave.

Bill pondered, "Am I denying Christ in some way by not telling them I am a Christian? Do I need to speak up?" He began to speak in Cantonese, and all eight of the security men from the PSB turned around and stepped back into the room. "However," Bill said out loud, "I am a Christian."

The director of the PSB shrugged his shoulders. "That's OK," he said. "We already know that. All of you Americans are Christians. We just don't want any missionaries coming into our country upsetting China's political system and trying to recruit the populace."

Obviously, the director's information about everyone in America being a Christian was somewhat skewed.

Within months, Bill became the official liaison for dozens of other medical organizations which had heard of the arrangements he had made with China. Everyone wanted in—and they began to contact Bill to intercede on their behalf as well. Samaritan's purse, Brother Andrew's Open doors, World Concern, as well as Orbis—an organization that recruited ophthalmologists who would donate their time, fly in and do eye surgery wherever they were needed.

Bill needed to get a better idea of small populations where work could be inserted, and the best way to do that was to take a roundtrip bus into areas that surrounded the city where he was staying. Throughout the day, buses ran a circular route into the countryside, going from village to village—ending back at their starting point then doing the same thing over and over again all day long.

He was shocked by the squalor. The remnants of extreme Communism continued to impose hardship on the people. Entire villages wore the Communist uniforms of gray and blue. Each village was a commune, expected to manufacture or grow everything they needed without any outside help. The system was primitive, ineffective, and brutal. Medical help was nonexistent, except for barefoot doctors with poor knowledge and minimal medical training.

Doing what he was doing alone, searching out small communities, meant that nobody knew where he was. It also meant that he had no way to get help if he got into trouble, or God forbid, into danger. He made a mistake one evening and got on the last bus of the day, not knowing that instead of circling back to the city, it might park up in the mountains. He wasn't expecting to spend the night in the bitter cold on an unheated bus not having a clue where he was.

The driver parked the bus and told Bill to get off. Bill shook his head, "No." The driver shrugged his shoulders and left. Bill had no idea what to do next. It was obvious he couldn't stay where he was and freeze. At that point, he was at the mercy of the bus driver and could only hope that he would come back and return to the city. But there was every possibility that he had parked the bus because his route for the day was finished.

After what seemed like an eternity, the driver did return. He started the bus without saying anything to Bill and began driving back to the city. On arrival, the driver flagged down a passing car and pointed for Bill to get in, which Bill thankfully did. He had no idea who the driver of the car was that took him back to his hotel. He could have ended up dead in an alley or a ditch.

He fell into bed and immediately was asleep, vowing never to get himself into a situation like that again. Naturally, that vow didn't last.

Chapter 43
Relief Funds

It was pitch black in the middle of the night when the boat pushed off the banks of the Saigon River with ten people on board. The boat should not have held more than six, but who could be left behind? The Vietnamese refugee who was trying to get his family on board to escape death couldn't make a choice like that.

Who would he leave? His wife? His three children? His aging parents—parents who had hidden and protected him and his family during the Vietnam war? Should he leave his brother, his brother's wife, and their baby son behind? No. If they died trying to escape the country, they would all die together. They were desperate to escape the carnage being inflicted by the fast-approaching North Vietnamese Army—who were killing all Vietnamese people who had supported the Americans.

By the time the refugee boat reached the islands of Macau, the baby had died from hunger, and both of the man's aging parents had passed away from dehydration. When the boat beached on the shore, locals called the police. It was a miracle that any of them had made it.

As the North Vietnamese Army had marched south, Boat People from Vietnam, who were trying to escape certain death, washed up on the shores of Macau. It was an everyday occurrence. The police transported what was left of each boatload of starving human flotsam to one of four Macau refugee camps.

The United Nations had worldwide guidelines for medical treatment of refugees. One of their rules was that you couldn't give refugees better treatment than you gave patients in the host country. It was one of the UN's many odd, unwieldy rules. Which meant that Bill couldn't go inside the refugee camps. Treating Vietnamese refugees inside the camp would mean that the American doctor who lived in Macau was giving preference to refugees over the local population. The ragged pitiful sick Vietnamese refugees had to step outside of the camp before Bill could examine them. Some were processed and approved for immigration to the United States. Or denied. It was a matter of examining them to determine if they had malaria, tuberculosis, syphilis, mental disorders, or some other problem—a problem that would disqualify them from immigration.

He treated them as they came to him. Clearing them for immigration if they met the requirements. Treating them for the diseases they carried with them into the country—many illnesses that couldn't be cured, which meant they would be denied any consideration for immigration.

Malnutrition, anemia, and filthy conditions caused most emigres bodies to be covered with abscesses—boils that had to be lanced. One twelve-year-old he treated was in very bad shape. Bill opened an infected wound on her sternum with a scalpel, poked a finger in to dig out the pus pockets, and found the infection had eaten a hole through the bone.

He had unknowingly run his finger through the hole in the sternum and into the heart, contaminating the entire area with the putrid infection drainage. He had introduced staph bacteria to the heart that was probably going to kill her.

He poured alcohol in the wound, injected her with penicillin because that was all he had, wrote up what had happened, and called his staff to pray. The next day, when he examined the child, there was no hole in the sternum and the wound was healed. Wounds like that don't heal overnight. Bone never heals like that; however, answers to prayer happened many times when a situation looked bleak. Faith in God to take care of what he couldn't became the norm for him and his staff. God did what God decided to do, and Bill did what he could.

He had seen miraculous recoveries before, but miracles are random—and always at the discretion of God himself. He had learned that while he was working as a resident at St. Johns in Tulsa. During the night, a woman with encephalitis had been unhooked by the interns from everything, except the respirator. Bacteria had eaten holes in her brain and liver; she had abscesses. The staff had been treating her with everything they had; her chances for survival were zero to none. Dilantin and phenobarbital had kept her in a coma to ease her suffering until she died.

Bill was doing rounds and felt impelled to touch the woman's forehead. He checked to make sure none of the accompanying residents were watching and would think he was a quack nut case. He asked God to heal her, the kind of prayer you don't really expect to be answered, knowing healing wouldn't happen. He didn't think about it again.

When Bill came to work the next day, the interns told him that all the tests on the woman that morning were normal; they had done them twice to be sure.

"You gotta' be kidding," Bill said. "Taper her off the meds. Let's see what happens."

They released her a few days later. EKG normal. Blood scan normal. Bacteria gone. She had been healed.

Bill got the message, "I'm God. You aren't. I am the one who decides. You are the one who prays."

Chapter 44
The Priest

The World Health Organization distributed funds to poverty-stricken clinics around the world, but the organization wouldn't give you funds for tuberculosis if the disease wasn't in your lungs—one more unreasonable WHO guideline. The lungs are almost always the first entry point of infection, but TB won't stay there. The lungs just pass it on, infecting the lymph, stomach, liver, skin, colon—anywhere it can get a hold in the body.

It was by far the most ravaging disease Bill dealt with in Macau. Thousands and thousands of people were infected. But by some miracle, he hadn't contracted TB even though he was exposed to it every day.

He had recently started working with Father Lancelot, a Catholic priest who had been allowed to stay in Macau as the Asian representative for the United Nations relief fund. All money coming in from the UN was funneled through Father Lancelot—and Lancelot was Julie's Fernandez's priest. The same Julie that worked as the international problem solver for Stanley Ho—the head of the Macau syndicate.

Julie told the priest that he needed to try and see if he could get Dr. Swan to help him with the distribution of the UN's relief funds. Julie had a unique knack for putting people together who needed to know each other. People from all over the world.

Bill was the only western doctor who had ever been allowed to practice at the Kiang Wu Communist hospital in Macau. And when Father Lancelot met Bill, he intuitively trusted his judgment and put him to work. He appointed him to be the Asian area representative for the UN Relief Fund for Medical Work, specifically for the Vietnam Boat refugee camps.

The priest needed help deciding where, and how, relief funds should be allocated. A Catholic priest and a Baptist missionary doctor working side by side was unusual, but they had a common mission and immediately became good friends.

Once again, Julie had hooked Bill up with someone who could help Bill do what he had come to Macau to do. When Father Lancelot saw what Bill had done for the Chinese refugees who had fled from the Red Guard, Lancelot immediately opened relief fund access to the refugee shanty town where people were living in huts made of wall-to-wall cardboard. It was a rabbit warren of packing slats and tin where the refugees were huddled.

Bill had been taking nurses in with him to try and attend to the overwhelming and critical medical needs of the refugees, but he had very limited financial resources to work with.

The entire mess of hovels had recently caught on fire and port authorities had taken a bulldozer to it—leaving hundreds and hundreds of people with nowhere to go. Father Lancelot began to dump whatever funds he could scrape together into rebuilding their shacks. He was horrified at the pitiful conditions, and overwhelmed with the task of feeding the helpless and homeless people.

Medical needs were almost impossible to deal with because you couldn't figure out where to start. The lack of medical care among refugees, homeless, and rural villages was appalling. Much of what Bill did began with teaching people basic skills—such as boiling water before you drank it, sanitation, nutrition, or not eating meat that wasn't properly cooked.

Starting a clinic always began from the ground up. Trying to tell people who were sick, starving, homeless, and desperate about Jesus always began with trying to help them first. Miserable, suffering people can't hear you. You have to help them first.

Chapter 45
Hopeless Conditions

Everywhere you looked in Macau, people were needlessly dying. The plethora of diseases was staggering. Before six months were behind him, the number of cases of tuberculosis that he was trying to manage never fell below seven hundred. Leprosy, malaria, typhoid, dengue fever, and syphilis had ravaged people—not to mention heart, kidney, liver, and lung diseases.

The only way Bill could find the help he needed was to train nurses himself; good medical help in Macau was nonexistent. He was the only western doctor in the country, and there wasn't enough of him to go around. He was exhausted. Sleep, when he could get sleep, was interrupted many nights by the latest emergency.

But by far, the most heart-wrenching part of the job was the Chinese orphanages where babies were chained inside cribs so that they couldn't crawl out. Others were placed in a room set apart for those infants who were dying or waiting to die—when their care was deemed hopeless by the stretched-thin, poorly trained staff. The only thing they were able to do was to leave the babies in the baby-dying room. Swaddled so that they couldn't move.

Every time a new missionary volunteer went into an orphanage, they were exposed to the dying babies. The volunteer's financial resources were allocated to form churches—permission from the IMB to spend your life working in an orphanage was funded only if you also worked with locals to create and found churches.

Organizing churches was the only way to find a permanent solution to make a change in the conditions of the orphanages. Not the other way around. It kept the missionaries under constant emotional stress. Not enough time; not enough money. With more unwanted babies coming into orphanages every day.

It was gut-wrenching, and some missionaries just couldn't do it. All they could see was the need, which meant that time and resources were always pulling them in opposite directions. Eventually, they were forced to compartmentalize their lives to be able to make it through the day—always trying to apply the words of the great preacher Oswald Chambers who said, "Every need is not a call." But the needs that surrounded them were always tugging them away from the call. The needs of the people presented a constant, suffocating, and all-consuming mental conflict.

Bill would continually remind himself that if he stopped at the cribs, he wouldn't have time to be able to effect any permanent change. He had to keep his focus on teaching the doctors and nurses what to do to alter the deplorable conditions. It ate him up. Some days it was an impossible task and he had to stop and comfort a baby—which meant his task of allocating his time to solve the permanent problem was deferred. It was like sticking one finger in a hole in the dike when there were dozens and dozens of holes still spewing water and tearing the dam apart.

Making time for his family was also a problem—he was torn in every direction—and his personal emotional health was going down the tubes. Morgan was already two years old; they had wanted more children, but after two years of trying, a miscarriage had left Janet brokenhearted. Bill saw so many dead babies every week, that it just seemed like one more dead baby, and he hadn't been able to grieve or express compassion appropriately to his wife.

"We'll keep trying," he told her. "There will be another baby."

It hadn't been enough. To Janet, it had been devastating. Not only had she lost the baby, but her husband seemed cold and uncaring. He was. He was breaking down. It would be two more years before their second son Matthew was born to heal the void left by her miscarriage.

Overwhelmed by helplessness in the middle of the unsurmountable need of the sick and dying, unable to decide which emergency to deal with next, Bill finally shut down completely. He quit getting up; he couldn't function. It was inevitable, a human disaster waiting to happen had just hit bottom. He couldn't even pray for help. He didn't know what to pray for first. Someone else was going to have to help him pick up the pieces of himself. PTSD had always been there. Lurking. Waiting. He was finally going to have to deal with it.

Three months of intensive Psychiatric rehabilitation in North Carolina—facing old fears of what might happen next when a pilot tried to land on the carrier and didn't make it. What might happen next to helpless babies in the China orphanages. What might happen next when TB was raging out of control all around him. What might happen next if he didn't get to deliver a pregnant mother in time. What might happen next if he didn't get lepers separated from their families before their families caught leprosy as well.

One man, trying to deal with catastrophes all by himself on every front. The list went on and on. He had tried to help all of the what-might-happen-next emergencies and had failed; he had never learned how to deal with failure. He had never faced his own limitations before. He had never had any limitations. Now, he did.

It took months of rehabilitation to rewire his thinking. To accept that there were some things that he couldn't fix. There were deaths that he couldn't prevent. He was going to have to prioritize his life and try to figure out where to start beginning again.

His breakdown was a wake-up call for the IMB. Their focus had been on starting churches, but after recognizing the success of the medical work Bill had initiated by setting up medical work in Macau and China, they finally realized that recruiting medical personnel to help him was critical.

Medicine was the vehicle that was opening doors, and Bill had to have people who could pick up some of the slack of that medical work—if he was going to have time to establish churches in restricted countries. He couldn't do it all. He certainly couldn't do it alone. The IMB needed a medical army. An army of people who were willing to go to jail if they were caught—with the possibility that they could die for the cause of Christ.

Chapter 46
Starting Over

Returning to Macau with a new realization of his own frailty, of his own inability to prevent the sickness and dying that surrounded him every day, Bill turned part of his time to the critical problem of recruiting nurses and doctors to help him at the clinic.

The Bowman Gray group had been able to penetrate the interior Chinese front, but Macau was where Bill lived and where he practiced medicine, and he couldn't keep everyone in Macau alive if he worked twenty-four hours a day. He was determined to spend more time with his family. And spend more time with other missionary families who had children—for the sake of his sons.

Realizing that the emotional health of their Asian missionaries had to be a priority, the IMB leased the top acreage of a small mountainous island between Macau and Hong Kong and built fourteen cabins as a retreat for families. There was a dining hall where they could eat and fellowship together. The men worked together and dammed a spring creating an ice-cold swimming pool. But the most important part of the retreat was that there was plenty of empty space for kids to run free.

Wild cattle inhabited the island, and of course, children chased them—against their parent's warnings. Morgan managed to rope one, tangle himself up in the rope, and was dragged away. Everyone began frantically yelling and hollering—finally catching the horned cow before Morgan was trampled or gored.

Such wild west cattle-rustling activities were not available for kids in the crowded, rat-infested, smog-ridden cities where people were crammed together in high rises, floor upon floor. At the retreat, children ran back and forth through the open landscape; it was impossible to corral them. Which was a good thing, even with an occasional frantic moment or two.

Bill started taking his guitar with him; he had discovered that some of the other guys had played with blue-grass combos when they were growing up. Every time the families got together, the men brought their instruments, perfected their skills, and began entertaining at events in Hong Kong—calling themselves 'The Nitty Gritty Lop Sop (garbage) Band', sporting straw hats and corn-cob pipes supplied by the folks back home.

The Chinese people loved the band's bluegrass rhythms and gave them standing ovations. Before long, they grew from three members to five, added drums and a soloist, and were tapped to play backup for Nashville bands that came to do shows in Hong Kong. The band got bigger and bigger reviews—until they were in such demand that it became difficult to balance their time. The Lop Sops had never dreamed of becoming a success as a band; they were just having some fun to balance the stress in their lives.

Eventually, they were forced to restrain themselves and limit their playing to missionary events. It took too much time to practice. They hadn't come to China to start a band.

He and Janet had started a church, and the people who came marveled that the doctor's Jesus-God didn't require sacrifices. The gods the people had been sacrificing to on Chinese New Year were evil. Those gods demanded gifts to appease them—gifts to keep the evil gods and their curses away.

The people were poor. They had nothing, and bringing gifts to the evil gods to keep from being persecuted—gifts of oranges, eggs, and other things they couldn't afford—was a heavy burden. One of the new Christians told Bill, "I'm free now. Jesus has paid my sacrifice, and I'm free."

Bill had learned a new, first-hand example of how to look at the scripture that said, "You will be free indeed."

Bill himself was healing. Learning to rearrange priorities in his life. Learning how to lie down at night, say his prayers, and go to sleep. Taking his boys to the missionary compound in Macau once a week to play with other kids who lived there.

He and Janet had moved back into their apartment on the 12th floor in Macau. But some of the medical people he had recruited chose to live inside the barbed wire safety of the IMB's fenced compound—where the stone walls were topped with ground glass to prevent break-ins. Macau wasn't safe. Anywhere. Ground glass didn't stop thieves; they just used gloves to protect their hands, then jumped over the fences.

The gardener who lived on the compound was named Louhbahk, 'Old Uncle' in English. He cultivated bonsai and raised dogs; the boys loved going to the missionary compound to play with Louhbahk's dogs. But sometimes, a dog the boys had grown fond of vanished. Bill finally got a clue—from the names that Louhbahk had given the dogs—which translated into English as 'Filet, Roast, or Chicken'. He hoped none of the missionaries living in the compound had unknowingly dined on one of the gardener's dogs—which, since it was China, was entirely possible.

Most of the time Bill navigated through the narrow streets of the old inner city on a motor scooter—where 16th-century buildings collapsed or burned on a regular basis. It was by God's grace that he didn't have one of the boys on his scooter the day a building collapsed on the road directly behind him—so close that the blast of the impact blew him sideways off the road.

The high rise they lived in was equally dangerous. Thieves watched the buildings to find out when an apartment was emptied to be renovated—so they could slip into it undetected, swing from the balcony to the balcony beneath, open the sliding doors of the occupied apartment, let themselves in, and take jewelry, money—or anything they could stuff in their pockets. If they were discovered, they would simply rappel down to the balcony below, or the next—until they found an empty room where they could let themselves inside to access the stairwell.

One of the agile invaders scaled down into Bill and Janet's apartment in the middle of the night and began rummaging around, making enough noise to wake Janet. She shook Bill and whispered, "Someone is in our living room!"

Bill picked up a plastic sword that the boys had been playing with that day. Armed with the toy sword, trying to be the man of the family, Bill was determined to attack the thief—who slipped out onto their balcony and swung to the balcony below. Nimble as a monkey.

The apartment thieves weren't dangerous. They had perfected their methods, carried no weapons, and reserved every empty space on their bodies to pack their loot. Stealing was an art form.

Chapter 47
Culture Shock

It wasn't their first experience with a thief. During their first week in Hong Kong, their apartment on the missionary compound was broken into. During the night, a thief used a glass cutter to carve a round hole in the glass door and slipped through the hole—just as Janet walked in the room on her way to the kitchen to get a glass of water. She screamed, and the thief calmly crawled back out the hole he had cut in the door. Thieves were for the most part non-violent. They were simply trying to make a living.

As if thieves weren't enough, the entire compound was besieged by rats. The week before they arrived, the caretaker had treated all the apartments using cardboard disks saturated with rat poison. He placed the flat poison disks in the corners of every room—and of course, two-year-old Morgan ate one—leaving a tell-tale sign of poison dust all around his mouth.

Bill frantically called the manufacturer of the disks to find an antidote; they assured him that the disks were harmless—explaining, "Don't worry; eating one of the disks won't hurt anyone. They don't even hurt the rats."

The company knew their product wouldn't kill rats. And that the Americans wouldn't know the difference. They also knew that the product would be in high demand for American compounds—due to the high population of the rats.

When Bill requested the names of the chemical compounds used in the disks, he realized that the poison was not poison at all. It was flour. Once again, someone was simply trying to make a living. One more Chinese anomaly—and an introduction to the Chinese version of capitalism in a Communist country.

Poisoning rats was a futile endeavor anyway; you couldn't keep track of which rats were actually dying. There were too many of them—dead and alive.

Rats reproduce at an alarming rate—there was no way to know if you were making headway on the rat population. They were outnumbered only by the mosquitos and termites. Swarms of both insects filled the air in such abundance that the air turned white. Nobody had warned the new missionaries to keep their windows closed. They learned that the hard way.

In 1976, when Bill and Janet arrived in country, Mao had been dead for two years, and the generals in the Red Army had taken over the mainland Chinese government. Hong Kong was still controlled by the British, but there was constant tension. Even though Janet had lived in Hong Kong for two years and thought she knew the territory, things had now changed since the Red Army had taken control of mainland China.

When they arrived, the couple had been ignorant about most things in the Chinese culture. They were isolated, alien foreigners, and constantly felt like they were under siege. Which they were. They needed time to learn how to live with it. It wasn't going to go away.

And to make things worse, Bill had a personality conflict with the treasurer of the Hong Kong mission. They butted heads over every expenditure. One of the other missionaries assured Bill that it wasn't him, the treasurer was constantly under pressure to stretch resources. But when the executive committee approved a budget item, Bill would have to spend money out of his own pocket, then present the receipt to the treasurer. It was always a struggle to get the treasurer to reimburse him.

Eventually, Bill bypassed the treasurer, went over his head to Richmond headquarters, and got paid—which made the Hong Kong treasurer furious. But Bill got what he needed; he did whatever was necessary to exist. He was well on his way to the Maverick Hall of fame.

At every turn, he met obstruction. His request for housing in Macau had been approved, but no one in the system had tried to find a place for them to live. He finally gave up and went to Macau by himself and began to search for a place for his family. He checked into a hotel, which meant that later he would have to go to war with the treasurer to get the hotel bill paid.

He left his wife and two sons on an island in Hong Kong in a one room wet concrete basement the mission had rented for them. They had been living there for months during Monsoon season; it rained every day. The roof leaked, the walls were wet and covered with mold, they had no transportation, no way to get groceries, and nowhere else to go—with their two young boys in the damp room day after day unable to go outside.

Conditions were already unbearable for his family—but after Bill left for Macau, a typhoon hit. He was stuck in the hotel unable to get back and get his family out. The executive committee was supposed to have found them a house in Macau. They didn't, and Bill was well on his way to learning that he was going to have to live on his own initiative. There simply wasn't enough funding or human support to solve every problem that a missionary had.

Chapter 48
Bloopers

"When you are sharing Christ in a language that is not your own, you are eventually going to mess up," Bill told the Asian IMB director. "The Conservative Baptists asked me to be the guest speaker at their denomination's conference. Their seminary is in Macau, and the conference is a big whoop-tee-doo for them.

"I assumed I was going to be speaking to a group of seminary leaders about TB cases in their student population. But when I walked into the room, it was packed with students who were already my TB patients, along with a convocation of visitors from mainland China—so I immediately changed my topic. I wasn't about to miss an opportunity to tell a Chinese audience about Christ—even though I hadn't prepared a sermon.

"My Cantonese is 100% accurate in the field of medicine; however, my religious vocabulary in Cantonese is probably only around 75%," Bill said. "When I was through speaking, accepting congratulations and appreciation, I was very pleased with the job I had done and my ability to speak the Cantonese language. Until one of the students asked me, 'Sir, why did you say that Jesus died on the duodenum—a part of the intestine? I thought he died on the cross.'"

That mistake permanently cured Bill's egotistical opinion of his Cantonese speaking skills.

Another speaking engagement humbled him even further. A driver picked him up in a blackout van, taking precautions to conceal him in case anyone was following. When the van stopped, the driver literally pushed him out the door and a stranger took hold of Bill's arm—leading him to an upstairs room packed with people. Bill thought he was going somewhere to talk to a group about rural health. But when he walked into the room, he realized that everyone had a Bible. Since meetings for religious purposes with Bibles were forbidden, what these people were doing was illegal. It was also very dangerous.

"Teach us," someone said to Bill. "Teach us how to justify obeying God while breaking the laws of our country at the same time."

Bill looked around the room and realized that answering this question could get someone killed since he couldn't actually verify that everyone in the room was a Christian; someone might report it. He jumped right in.

"We obey man's law unless it violates God's laws," Bill told them. Then asked, "Have any of you ever known someone who was arrested because they were a Christian?" He was shocked when half the room raised their hands. "Have any of you personally been arrested?"

One-third of the people in the room raised their hands. He was in awe. These people were already endangering their lives. This meeting was nothing new for them. The very least he could do was teach them and endanger his own life as well. He began to teach.

Due to his success in setting up medical facilities, other organizations started contacting him and moving into the areas that Bill had opened up. Samaritan's Purse, Christian Missionary Alliance, as well as the Presbyterians and Nazarenes. The Chinese government realized that the medical system that Bill had started was a good deal for them, and began to allow groups in who would promise to build hospitals or schools. China was now on the take.

Most Christian association members in other organizations and denominations called the Baptists 'Cadillac missionaries' because their missionaries were totally funded. They didn't have to stump for money. Other religious groups had to raise money back in the states for everything they did, so they were regularly trying to get Bill to volunteer and help them out.

One of them asked Bill if he would go up north to Zhao Tong with a physician from their organization. If such a request looked like it might be a way for Bill to get a foothold in an area to start a clinic, he was glad to help. But the doctor that invited Bill to go with him to Zhao Tong had another agenda—and wasn't totally up-front about it. He wanted to build a private medical school. He wanted to make some money.

The Baptist IMB wasn't going to help fund the construction of a hospital in a rural area—much less a medical school, so the trip seemed destined to be a waste of Bill's time. To make it even worse, the weather was horrendously cold. As the bus they were on climbed a narrow mountain road, they encountered a horrible wreck that had caused a landslide. Vehicles had tumbled off over the side of the mountain; people were dead, others were trapped in their cars and freezing at the bottom of the cliff—beyond the reach of people on the road. It was going to take rescue equipment.

When the two men didn't show up at their destination, the people waiting on them in Zhao Tong became so concerned that they sent a bus to find out what happened. As the bus pulled to a stop, stranded people who could still walk scrambled to get on. Rob and Bill got the last two seats under an open hole in the roof of the bus, a bus so rickety that it should have been condemned.

As the road to Zhao Tong climbed higher, the temperature dropped lower and the snow increased, falling through the hole in the roof onto Bill and Rob. When they finally arrived at a place where they could stay, they were so bitterly cold that a local Chinese general took them to his own home—afraid that the two Americans were going to freeze to death, and that it would cause an international incident. He built a fire to keep them warm, fed them hot soup, gave them army issue coats, and got them a government car.

Once they thawed out, the two men hired a guide for the rest of their trip to Zhao Tong—a college professor who taught English as a second language and was an interpreter on the side. He was curious about the Americans and asked why they had come. Bill explained that he was a Christian—a servant of Jesus Christ—and that he wanted to help people know about what Jesus had done for them.

"Who is this Jesus person?" the man asked Bill. The guide had never met a westerner or a Christian. Neither had anyone else in the area.

Bill told the guide the story about Jesus and explained why God had sent Jesus to earth.

"This is wonderful news!" the guide exclaimed. "How long have you known this!"

"I've known it all my life," Bill told him. "Jesus came over two thousand years ago."

"Where have you been? Why hasn't anyone come here to tell us about this?" The guide was visibly distressed. "My father died last week," he cried. "He didn't get to hear this wonderful news!"

Bill spent the rest of the time they were heading north on the road to Zhao Tong teaching his guide about Christ. But even though the interpreter accepted the Lord and promised to tell others, Bill felt like he was scraping the surface, scattering seed and hoping for the best—because he knew he would never return that way, or see the guide again.

Encountering people who had never heard about Christianity was not unusual. He was thankful for the opportunities that God set up, but had to hope that someone else would water what was planted. He knew it wouldn't be him. Someone else would have to follow up. He was already stretched thin.

Three years later his prayer was answered when the IMB funded a permanent missionary to the area. He found the guide that Bill had introduced to Christ and baptized him along with all of his family.

Chapter 49
Dangerous Encounters

Every day it was something different. The Chinese provincial government asked him to visit one of their hospitals which was located in a rural area. He accepted the invitation, even though the hospital building was suspect—it looked like a cheap drive-in motel. Each patient was housed in an individual room with their door opening to the outside. When he finished with one case, he had to step out of that room to get to the patient in the next room.

A crowd began to gather around him, wanting to touch him, curious about the round-eyed white American doctor. None of them had ever seen a westerner before. They grabbed at the papers he was carrying—trying to look at the strange scribbles he had made. Pushing and shoving him. The throng of people grew so large that he couldn't get away from them to enter the next patient's room. Trapped and smashed against the wall of the building—he was unable to move.

Someone must have called the police because an ambulance drove in right through the middle of the mob. Two men grabbed him, literally threw him through the back doors of the truck, and took off—with the crowd following close behind. He was scratched and bruised, but still in one piece—thankful for the rescue.

"I'm willing to see your patients," Bill told the authorities. "But you have to give me protection or I'm not going to be able to do the job."

It was the first time he felt like he had been in real danger, but it wasn't the last. He was about to witness an assassination.

Chapter 50
Syndicate Wars

In an attempt to fund the government in Macau, Portugal decided to issue contracts requiring a license to run a casino business—offering contracts to the Chinese, Triads, Americans, or anyone else who had an interest. The Portuguese government in Macau had decided that taking control of licensing for the casinos could be an untapped taxation method for covering their government's expenses.

Stanley Ho had enjoyed a monopoly on casinos from the git-go; he was not going to give up control of them without a fight—a war was inevitable. The day the requirement for a license was signed by the Portuguese, Stanley, the Chinese Triads, and American enterprises with interests in gambling casinos began to fight over who would be in charge of the lucrative empire that made Macau the gambling center of the world. Who would get the government's casino contracts? That was the big question.

The Chinese Triads immediately began to assassinate their opposition as they tried to gain control. They even broke into the government compound and set fire to every single police motorcycle—giving notice to the government as well as the police: "Don't interfere." It was the beginning of a war much like the one between Al Capone and Elliott Ness in America—but much bloodier, and significantly more powerful.

The Triads already controlled graft in 'China-towns' in many other parts of the world. Vancouver, San Francisco, Los Angeles, and New York. The U.S. wasn't about to try to cover policing in those American China-towns. They immediately bowed out of the conflict for the contract on the Macau casinos—leaving the Triad mobs positioned to take over from Stanley Ho.

Stanley Ho had always taken care of any difficulties he encountered through a second or third party. He may have been a crook, but he did things clean—with no 'in-your-face' violence. Now, that was no longer possible. Murder was rampant on all fronts. Including murder for hire.

In an effort to control the Triads, the Macau government pulled in a special team of experts from mainland Portugal to clean things up and restore control. Their suggestions on how to manage the problem only lasted one week before those Portugal government experts were assassinated.

Headed to work one morning on his scooter, Bill stopped at a red light. As he was waiting, a motorcycle pulled up next to him and a man with a gun opened fire on the Portuguese government's car in the next lane—killing everyone in the vehicle. Two Portuguese officials in the front seat and one in the back.

Bill was panicked, but the assassin ignored him—as well as everyone else who witnessed what had just happened. The killer was across the border and back into China before the Macau police could start looking for him. At that point, the Portuguese government bowed out. Macau could take care of its own problems.

"How do you expect me to do medical work in an atmosphere like this?" Bill asked the authorities. "My people that work in the clinic are frightened. They're worried; my wife is worried. We're all scared."

"You don't need to worry about the Triads," the government agent assured him. "There is nothing for you to be afraid of. Those people are excellent shots, and they know who they are after. They know exactly who they want to take out, and they are very good at what they do. They know we won't interfere because if we do, they will target us as well. They just want their enemies dead. They have no interest in harming either you or the rest of the public."

Chapter 51
Portuguese Trouble

In addition to the war between Stanley Ho and the Triads, problems with the Portuguese government over his medical license continued to plague Bill as well. It had been an uneasy alliance since day one. The Portuguese had not given up on getting him out of Macau and had served notice that he was going to be evicted within a month.

They did not want him there because he had not followed their procedures and rules for getting a medical license in Macau. He had bucked their authority. The Portuguese wanted to be sure that everyone knew that they were the ones who had the power to enforce regulations and that they were going to do it. They couldn't control Stanley Ho or the Triads, but they could certainly control Bill.

Julie Fernandez had great influence on the local government but had not been able to get them off of Bill's back. The government's newest tactic was to deny the renewal of his medical license and shut down his clinic. The only way for Bill to get around being thrown out of Macau was to obtain a permanent license from the European mother-country of Portugal itself. But Portugal didn't have a medical reciprocity agreement with the United States.

Julie, the world traveling secretary of the syndicate's head Mr. Stanley Ho, had connections. She knew somebody. She knew a lot of somebodies. Worldwide. And she believed in the righteous work Bill was doing. She might be a mob boss liaison, but she was also a good Catholic girl.

Julie suggested that Bill contact Alecia Alverez, the wife of the Attorney General in a country that spoke Portuguese. Alecia had a Ph.D. in international law. In contrast with her humble beginnings, she was very sophisticated, dressed to the nines, and had the skills and the chutzpa to tear into any international office that treated people unfairly.

Alecia had been living in abject poverty when a Baptist missionary to Brazil recognized Alecia's potential and took her under her wing. The missionary paid for Alecia's college education and gave her an unexpected and bright future. Alecia never forgot.

She was fueled with a strong incentive to use her law degree to help the Baptist's International Mission Board with its legal problems—problems that were consistently tangled up in international confusion. She volunteered her legal services to the IMB and offered her expertise to help straighten out any legal difficulties that they might have.

When she heard about the problem Bill had encountered as he was trying to get the Portuguese to renew his medical license in Macau, she got on a plane, flew to Portugal, and marched into Lisbon's Medical University. Fluent in the Portuguese language, she was able to clearly communicate what she wanted—and used her knowledge of international law to fix Bill's problem.

She left Europe with a Portuguese Medical license for Bill, along with an honorary diploma in his name from the Lisbon Medical University. An honorary diploma with honors. No qualms over the fact that Bill not only hadn't graduated from Lisbon University, he hadn't ever stepped foot inside the country of Portugal. Alecia Alverez was a force to be reckoned with, and Bill's problems with the Portuguese government's colony in Macau were over and done with. He had a license to practice medicine from the Portuguese. Signed, sealed, and delivered.

However, getting a medical license in Hong Kong was a different problem altogether and Bill had hit a brick wall there. Great Britain, which had sovereignty in Hong Kong, wouldn't reciprocate a medical license with the United States.

They were probably still miffed over the fact that they had been on the losing side of the American Revolution—which made them look like number two in the world. They considered themselves far superior to any other nation on the planet—with nothing to back it up but pomposity. Royal superiority. They would, however, reciprocate with Manitoba, Canada, which was part of the British Empire. Just not with the United States.

Bill submitted an application for a medical license in Manitoba, a Canadian province, then flew there to take their medical exam. When the Manitoba medical authorities saw that he had an American license, they said that he didn't need to take the test. It wasn't necessary because their exam was identical to the United States' exam. They automatically approved him. Britain didn't. They said he had to actually, physically, take the boards in Canada.

He had already returned home to Macau when he heard the news. He turned around, flew back to Manitoba, took the exams, passed, then mailed the Canadian certification to England. The British said no. They wouldn't give him a British license. Since Bill lived in Macau, he must be Asian; he would have to prove that he could speak proper English.

"I'm writing to you in proper English!" he told them. "I've spoken to you over the phone in proper English! I am a proper English-speaking American citizen!"

It didn't matter. The British had some need to prove something to American medical applicants. Medical applicants from America needed to recognize that England was superior to the rest of the world. Bill was informed that he had to physically go to London and take an oral English exam to prove he was fluent in English.

However, they did finally bend and said that in lieu of flying to London to take the oral exam, they would accept a document proving that he had already practiced medicine in the English language for five years inside America where American doctors spoke the King's English.

Bill called Don Collins, the hometown Pryor physician he had worked with while he was waiting for the IMB to approve him for the mission field. "You're not going to believe this!" he told Don.

Bill explained all the hoops he had jumped through trying to get a Hong Kong license and told Don about the letter he had to have from a licensed American physician. A letter to authenticate that he had practiced medicine for five years in the English language. This was a perfect opportunity for Dr. Collins to improvise as a comedian. Which he did. With gusto.

He wrote: "Dr. Swan not only practiced in the English language for well over five years, but he is a wonderful Indian boy (Bill didn't have a drop of Indian blood) who speaks fluent Cherokee, Osage, Choctaw, and every other known Indian language in addition to English. He is an honorary Indian chief in the great state of Oklahoma, acting as the English language interpreter for all of the Indian Nations with the Bureau of Indian Affairs in Washington."

Don rambled on with similar fabrications for two more pages.

"Tell me you didn't send that!" Bill yelled at him over the phone.

"I thought it was a masterpiece," Don said. "I can't believe you didn't like it."

"OK, you've had your fun. Send me a copy of the one you actually sent to the British. And so help me, it better be good."

Of course, it was, and Bill finally had his license to practice in England. But he still had to present the medical authorization from Great Britain to the Hong Kong government and wait for Hong Kong to approve it. He had been in Macau for three years before he also got his medical license in Hong Kong.

He now was legally licensed to practice medicine in the United States, Macau, China, Canada, Hong Kong, and Great Britain. However, he vowed he would never again waste his medical skills on the British unless they got on their knees and begged.

Chapter 52
Finding Help

The medical work in Macau had grown to the point that Bill couldn't cover it; he was constantly trying to find help. He needed help, but help was difficult to find—much less keep. One of the internists Bill had recruited to come to the mission field became so frustrated with learning the Cantonese language that he had resigned and gone back to America.

However, Bill knew that medical school students in the United States were required to do a three-month preceptorship with a practicing physician at the end of their fourth year of Med school. They could do it anywhere, and many of the students looked at Bill's invitation to do the three-month stint in Macau as an adventure and were excited for the opportunity to help him.

He was more than willing to take them—even if it was for only three months. He needed help and the students were eager. They were fun for him to be around—in a country where Americans were few and far between. It was nice to have someone to work with who spoke English—and wasn't British.

One student that applied to join him was a Korean-American. When the state department got wind of it, they said, "No," the student couldn't come—because a Korean restaurant two doors down from Bill's clinic was an undercover Korean spy training camp. The state department feared the student would be kidnapped.

Bill appealed and convinced the Department of Foreign Affairs that he had excellent relations with the Triads and Stanley Ho and that nobody in Macau would ever kidnap a Korean-American citizen or they would end up dead. He argued that it would give the student excellent experience working in a foreign country. The approval came with the stipulation that Bill or Janet had to be with the student at all times. It was difficult to do, but worth it to have an extra hand in the clinic for three months.

He never found out why the state department thought the young man might be kidnapped. Or why the Koreans were running a spy training camp in Macau. Neither made any sense. But there were many things in Macau that didn't make sense.

Trying to recruit doctors to work with him had become more and more urgent. He needed doctors, but he also needed them to assist with the primary mission of sharing the gospel. Even though it meant leaving the clinic for a few days, the need to find medical personnel was so critical that he flew to Los Angeles or San Francisco every few months. It became a necessary and regular part of his routine.

The Oriental churches along the California coastline welcomed him, setting up conferences and speaking engagements so that he could explain the work he was doing in Hong Kong and Macau. He was able to share the desperate need for volunteers.

Native Korean and Chinese students from nearby universities spread the word about the American missionary doctor from Macau, and as his conference attendance grew, so did his success in reaching Christian students who were in medical school.

Chapter 53
Martyrdom

The strategy coordinator for North Korea had asked Bill to help him find and recruit a Korean doctor, and although there were a number of Korean Americans who were very interested in serving as missionaries in East Asia, Bill always made sure that they knew how perilous it was—the dangers were extreme—and Bill was careful to clearly spell out those dangers.

This kind of work was not an adventure. It could be deadly, and when he was trying to recruit someone, Bill stressed those dangers. To make sure volunteers understood, he would share the story of a Korean American cardiologist from Virginia Beach.

The Virginia Beach doctor had jumped right into covert missionary work, training other Korean Christians to share the gospel undercover. He had moved into a house in Russia, right next to the North Korean border, and set up an infiltration group to take the message across the border, warning them that the need for secrecy was critical. Sometimes they were able to help North Korean people escape and cross into Russia, but sometimes the undercover Christians agents didn't make it back out.

If they were able to get people out of North Korea and into Russia, they could then cross into China. They were given instructions to look for places with the number ten on the doorpost. In the Korean language, the number ten was a cross—and even though the Koreans couldn't speak Mandarin or Cantonese, the symbol of the cross on the doorpost would let them know that the building housed a Christian Church where they would be safe.

The Virginia Beach doctor was so effective that the North Korean government made a concentrated effort to catch him—and eventually, their agents discovered where he lived. Assassins broke into his house, murdered his wife and children, and when he returned home, tortured and killed him as well. The North Korean government was committed to murdering Christians who gave allegiance to a higher power than their leader. It was a huge loss for undercover missions in the Korean Christian community.

Bill carried a heavy burden as he recruited people to go into restricted countries through the underground. Sometimes, when one of them didn't come back, you knew they were in prison or had been killed. Some of them simply vanished and were never heard from again. Martyrs, who knew exactly what the dangers were in East Asia for telling people about Christ—yet were still willing to die to share His story.

In spite of the warnings about what could happen, volunteers continued to surrender their lives to missions. Medical help trickled in, along with nurses and more and more Asian-Americans who knew what the cost might be to go into restricted countries and tell people about Jesus.

Chapter 54
Culture Shock

The people he recruited always experienced culture shock. Doctors, nurses, medical students, and missionary hopefuls were unprepared for the conditions they encountered.

"You'll have to carry those bags yourselves," Bill told a group of nurses who had brought their own food packed in extra suitcases. "There won't be any help at the gate to assist you. You might think about leaving your food in your rooms and eating local cuisine."

That wasn't going to happen. The nurses had heard stories from people who attended conferences back in the states where Bill had shared information, "If you go to a movie, you won't get popcorn and coke. All the theaters serve rat on a stick. Much like a corn-dog."

Bill had been eating on the street ever since he arrived in the Orient. He never asked what it was that he was eating. He had eaten more than rats. If you attended a banquet, you ate what your host gave you, and they always gave you something they knew would be offensive to an American, just to watch the reaction.

Earthworms, roasted scorpions, sparrows, toasted maggots, dog, cat, turtle, snake, pigeons, fish eye soup—he had eaten it all. It was rude to refuse to eat what you were served, and if you wanted to get your foot in the door and establish a medical clinic in the area, you ate what they gave you. When it was something Janet couldn't stomach, she would quietly slide it onto Bill's plate. The Chinese whispered behind Bill's back, "The American doctor has the stomach of a goat."

Some hosts would taunt the recruits that Bill brought with him. "If you don't share my food and drink with me, I don't want to be friends with your Jesus man."

So, Bill and the recruits ate and drank whatever they gave you—and if it was fermented, you didn't report your transgression to the IMB. Baptists had strong feelings about alcohol. The IMB wouldn't understand beer in the name of Jesus. You simply never asked what it was they served you. It was easier to swallow if you didn't ask and didn't know.

For first-timers to Macau or China, dining out was unsettling. The sound of rats scratching and running through the walls and ceilings was their dinner music. And cats, both under, as well as on top of the tables, were the clean-up crew. Eating out was one of those, "When in Rome do as the Romans do" kind of adjustments—without the refinement of Rome.

Far Eastern Asia had a flavor all its own, and you needed to have a strong stomach to eat the food. It was not uncommon for a recruit to lose twenty pounds during their two-week stay. One of them remarked that if God hadn't called you to the mission field in East Asia, you would never have come.

And of course, Bill occasionally made mistakes. On one trip, he had forgotten and let his visa expire. "Come with me," the gate attendant told him.

Bill was apprehended as he and those he had brought with him exited the country. He left two frightened medics who were unable to speak the language in a waiting room; they were terrified. The attendant took him to a back room, gave him a lecture, then stamped his visa and warned him never to do that again. The two medics he had brought into China with him never volunteered to return and help him again.

Cultural differences were always of great interest to the volunteers he brought in with him. In the mountains of China, Yao women had huge mounds of hair on their heads. They practiced ancestor worship in a unique way by cutting the hair of their dead, passing down generations of their ancestor's hair, and weaving into their own. Once a month they had a hair-washing ritual that all of the women practiced together at a small brook.

Recruits were always shocked when they saw young children—as young as six and seven—running through streets and alleys smoking cigarettes. And shocked at the number of babies sitting in baskets on the street with a note pinned to them, "Take me with you."

Usually, the babies were girls—or boys that were deformed.

China had a rule that you could only have one child per family, and it affected which child a parent kept and which one was discarded, since most families wanted boys. Not only were girls considered to be inferior, but the

Chinese culture held boys responsible for taking care of their parents as they grew old. After a girl married, she was expected to help care for the parents of her husband. Having a girl as your only child held no permanent advantage. Get rid of the girl—put her in a basket on the street, and try again for a boy.

Those missionary recruits who were used to taking a bath every day were also in for a shock. Showers weren't always available, especially in the winter—and when they were available, hot water was only on tap from nine to ten in the evening for one hour. There wasn't enough time for everyone to take a hot shower.

When recruits traveled, a train's sleeping car had to be shared with strangers. "You have to sleep in the compartment with the American devil," was a common phrase Bill overheard. The Chinese had no idea that Bill could understand their language and that he knew what they were saying. One group said, "Put grandma in with the foreign devils. If they kill her, it won't matter. She's going to die soon anyway."

Chinese villagers swarmed the American doctors, begging to have their picture taken with them. Bill obliged and would give away the Polaroid image. You never knew when it might help you make a contact. He smiled for the camera—which the Chinese didn't do. The Chinese were sober-faced and totally serious. They had never owned a picture.

He was always welcome in small villages because he spoke the common man's language—Cantonese. Those who spoke Mandarin were suspect; Mandarin was the language that business people usually spoke—those who sought to take financial advantage of the people.

Chapter 55
Breaking Rules

The Bowman Gray flow of doctors continued volunteering for two-week medical excursions into mainland China. The Chinese had elevated Bill to V.I.P. status, and every time there was an exchange of equipment or doctors, they threw a banquet in his honor and treated him like royalty.

The only problem with the high-profile special treatment he received from the Chinese was that the International Mission Board had not approved him to enter China. He hadn't asked permission, which was a no-no. China was a restricted country. You had to have IMB headquarters' permission—and Bill wasn't about to ask and be refused.

However, he did inform the local Asian IMB director what he was doing—just in case something went wrong. The director warned him that there were two things he absolutely could not do or they would both get in trouble.

"Don't get arrested," he told Bill. "And don't let anyone take your picture. I don't particularly want to be implicated in your illegal shenanigans."

The IMB wasn't the only one that didn't know what Bill was doing. The American Embassy had only recently discovered that he had been going into mainland China. America's Secretary of State, Cyrus Vance, phoned the American Embassy in Hong Kong wanting to know who this loose-gun rogue William Swan was.

Secretary Vance wanted to know exactly how Doctor Swan was getting into China, why he was going into a Communist country, and what he was doing while he was there. Vance hadn't approved it, and you absolutely didn't go into a restricted country without permission from Vance.

The American Embassy in Hong Kong began a scramble to find out what was going on with the unruly American who was crossing the border into China. They began an in-depth investigation.

The fact that the Hong Kong Embassy served as the undercover Asian headquarters for the CIA was a poorly kept secret. Bill had not only come under the direct scrutiny of Cyrus Vance, America's head of the state department but the CIA as well.

While trying to avoid investigation by the American government, Bill was trying to be very careful to avoid the two things the Asian missionary director for the IMB had warned him about as well; the director had stuck his neck out for Bill by not reporting what he was doing, and Bill didn't want either himself or the director to get into deeper trouble with IMB headquarters.

The first thing the director told him he couldn't do was to get arrested, which was always a possibility if the Chinese discovered Bill's real intentions for crossing the border. However, Bill thought there would be no problem with the second thing the director had told him—concerning someone taking his picture. The general Chinese public didn't have cameras.

There hadn't been a problem with pictures until the Chinese honored Bill with second-row seats at the Cantonese Opera in Guang Jou, and Ted Kennedy, along with an entourage of his people, sat down directly in front of Bill—accompanied by a swarm of photographers. Bill and Janet's faces were in almost every photograph that was taken.

The International Mission Board and the US Secretary of State, Cyrus Vance, might not have sanctioned Bill being in China, but God must have approved of the work he was doing—because the pictures were never published in America and the CIA didn't get a copy.

The Chinese approved of him being in their country helping them get doctors to teach them Western medical practices. The fact that the IMB as well as the American government didn't approve was a minor inconvenience.

Chapter 56
Clinic Relief

People in churches across America had become aware of the missionary in Macau called the Macau Maverick, a nickname he had earned because of his penchant for disobeying rules. His picture and nickname had appeared on the front cover of the Baptist Messenger—a publication that made its way into almost every Baptist home across the nation.

Church members, who tithed ten percent of their income to their churches, had questions. Why didn't the IMB have work inside China? Laos? Cambodia, and other Asian countries. Information had recently been released that 94% of the people who had never heard the gospel message were in countries with restricted access, but almost all of the Baptist missionary funding was going to countries where you could already openly share the gospel. It didn't make sense.

Since official IMB policy was that no missionaries would be inserted into restricted countries, Bill simply didn't share with the IMB that he was escorting doctors from Bowman Gray into the mainland. Or that he was Bowman's official liaison with Asia. No need to cause a problem where one didn't yet exist.

The IMB decision on restrictions was based on three things. First, there were a number of opposing religions that didn't allow Christians into their bally-wick—Christians were considered heretics who were worthy of death. Second, there were some places where the geographical conditions—such as jungles or mountainous terrain—made it impossible to travel.

And third, there was the danger of imprisonment—some foreign governments didn't want their citizens to give allegiance to some higher authority in their lives. But China had become big news, and church members began to clamor that danger wasn't a legitimate reason for not spreading the gospel into restricted places.

Baptists were proud of their distinction as a Christian denomination. One, they believed in missions overseas. And two, they were tithers—giving ten percent of their income to their churches, who in turn gave a part of what came in each month to their International Mission Board—the IMB. Church members began to pressure the mission board to change their policy on restricted countries. Church members wanted their tithes to count.

The consensus of the IMB was to agree—they needed to go where they were most needed—to the 94% of the world who had never heard about Christ; who had never heard the gospel story. But how were they going to get into areas where they were forbidden to go? And how were they going to go about funding the work in those restricted areas?

The solution was to form a new secret organization-within-an-organization that would function independently. An organization that would never be identified or recognized as a religious entity. Its sole purpose would be to insert Christians into restricted countries. They named the organization Cooperative Services International, CSI—a secular corporation that would distribute funds from its small nondescript storefront headquarters in London. Not only would missionaries be undercover, the IMB itself was now going undercover to fund CSI—which in turn would fund the missionaries.

Chapter 57
Going Rogue

Bill wanted in. He was itching to get into this new operation. Being able to get into a place he wasn't supposed to go was right down his alley. But first, he had to find a replacement for the huge medical work he had created in Macau—work that had spread like the tentacles of an octopus reaching into China.

He was now the East Asian medical consultant responsible for the health care of over a thousand missionaries and volunteers in various positions. Once a year they all met at a conference in Chiang Mai in the mountains of northern Thailand. He tested blood, dispensed medications, and immunized their children—all of which, including his own sons, had some degree of lead poisoning. It took a crew of medical workers to get that done, but the responsibility to see that it was all done was his.

He doubled down on his efforts to find someone who could take over the work in Macau—with no luck. Instead, that unrecruited and undiscovered someone found Bill.

When the clinic phone rang, a doctor by the name of Keith from Louisiana said, "Doctor Swan, I've heard about your work. I think that God wants me to come to Macau and work with you. The only thing holding me back is that I need some assurance that there are parks and outdoor places for me and my family to spend time. We're big on the outdoors."

"Then don't come to Macau, it's not the place for you. Thanks for calling," Bill said. And hung up.

He was so busy working at the clinic training nurses and recruiting American doctors as the middle-man broker for the hospital in Guang Jou, that he didn't have time for wanna-be inquirers taking up his time on the phone. People often called who weren't suited for the crammed, thirty or forty-story high-rise buildings infested with rats, pollution, and millions of people. Macau certainly didn't provide parks and recreation facilities for families. No point in encouraging someone to move to Macau when they wouldn't make it—and would subsequently resign.

One month later, Keith called back. "God won't let go of me," he said. "We're coming to Macau."

Within months, Keith and his family moved into a small apartment on the 35th floor of a high-rise that swayed from side to side with every incoming typhoon. He would faithfully serve there for thirty years—taking over and expanding the work that Bill had created in Macau.

Once Keith arrived, Bill immediately joined Cooperative Services International—CSI. He moved his family to Hong Kong and prepared to go completely undercover and begin working only in restricted Asian countries.

He joined a new group of younger hot-shot missionaries who had been dubbed 'James Bonds with Bibles', and began indoctrinating them into the intricacies of how to get across closed borders—an activity he had already perfected. Everything they did was secret. Communications were in coded messages, and they lived with the realization that if they were caught, they would be thrown out of the country, or God forbid, they would be jailed or killed.

Bill had recently been caught smuggling Bibles by one of the provincial outlying rural governments in China—and the country of China had blacklisted him. He had lost his ability to get back into the country and as a result, his connections with the hospitals in China were lost. Bowman Gray was still able to continue their exchange of doctors that Bill had set up, however, missions in China were now out of the picture for him. Or so it would seem, but he had a plan to get around that problem.

He was going to become anonymous. All he needed was a new identity and a new passport. He would never be able to get back across the border with his current identification since the Chinese hand-checked passport numbers at every entry point.

He solved the problem by applying for a new passport—and along with his new passport, he was issued a new number. Since there was no computerization at the time, the passport was untraceable, and he continued to cross into China with a new name and passport number. He was now a ghost.

He eventually obtained three different passports. Passports always presented problems if you wanted to travel in East Asia. Taiwan would not accept his U.S. passport because it had a Chinese stamp. Taiwan had declared themselves independent of China during a war—a situation which China refused to acknowledge or accept. Other areas had equally frustrating rules. And of course, he had to have his legitimate passport to travel between Asia and America.

Everything a CSI underground missionary member planned to do—when they left their headquarters in Hong Kong—had to be done under someone else's name. Bill was now a 'persona non grata' moving undetected through East Asia. Protected only by the grace of God.

Chapter 58
Mongolia

Excursions into restricted countries during the 1970s were always a toss-up. You never knew whether you could get back out or not. You also never knew how you were going to be able to travel into the country's interior once you got in. Donkey, camel, ox-cart, motorcycle, bicycle, unreliable broken-down Jeep, or on foot. A bus was Bill's favorite mode of transportation. In China, you could board a bus, ride around its route traveling in a circular loop and get the lay of the land you were in. But a bus would not be possible in Mongolia.

When Bill got off the plane in Mongolia, the temperature was forty below zero. It was February, the middle of winter. Anyone who stayed outside in the cold would freeze the inside surface of their lungs. The instant he exhaled; his breath froze on contact with the air. It was the coldest cold he had ever experienced in his life.

His single protection was a military issue hood lined with wolverine which was the only known fur that wouldn't ice up in subzero weather when you breathed. He wore a down expedition jacket, or he wouldn't have survived. Even then, when he arrived in country, he had to buy more clothes and blankets to be able to endure the trip he was about to take heading north.

He had expected to pick up his bags in the terminal when he arrived, but the airline attendant threw his bags out of the plane onto the tarmac, where his suitcase hit the runway like a rock and the wheels broke off. He dragged his bag into a one room primitive shack that served as a terminal and waited in line for an hour and a half just to buy a loaf of bread.

Mongolia was the only country in East Asia where you had to have two visas. One visa to get in, and another one to get back out. Conditions were primitive. Conditions were also unbearable. But he was on a mission. Mongolia needed medical help. And he had a gospel message to share.

No Christian had lived in Mongolia in the country's history—a country that had only recently declared its independence from Russia. Since he didn't speak either Mongolian or Russian, Bill found a guide with a dilapidated Jeep who spoke both languages as well as broken Cantonese.

"Can you get me north?" he asked the man.

Mongolia's Minister of Health had heard about Bill's work in China and had asked if Bill would come and help them train doctors and set up a 'rural' health system. Getting an official invitation was an unexpected foot in the door. After meeting with the director at the airport, Bill and his guide headed North to check out the medical conditions in the freezing rural areas—where the death rate for new-born babies was reported to be over sixty-seven percent.

Setting up a rural health system in this frozen terrain was going to be almost impossible since Mongolia had no general practitioners to run them. Compounded by the fact that 'rural' communities didn't actually exist.

If you didn't live in one of the five small cities in Mongolia, it was because you were a sheep herder in the Steppes—where entire families lived year-round and slept in yurts—circular structures which were easily taken down when the herders pulled up stakes to move and find new grass for their animals. No real villages or permanent settlements existed—these people were constantly on the move from place to place with their horses and goats.

As Bill and his guide moved north, the terrain proved almost impossible for the Jeep to navigate, and places to buy food were nonexistent. When the driver ran out of supplies, he improvised by finding and cooking road kill on a butane burner he carried with him in the Jeep—you'll eat anything if you are hungry enough.

Eventually, they stumbled onto one of the nomad groups—at the exact moment the crankshaft failed and the Jeep died. They were lost at that point anyway.

That night, Bill thanked God for a place to sleep out of the freezing cold—in a yurt with an obliging family who shared their fermented goat milk curd for supper. It was an improvement over road-kill.

He had learned one thing from the excursion: the possibility of rural health care for these people was impossible—because you would never be able to find them. Medicine was not going to be able to go to them; nomads were going to have to travel to some type of regional medical facility themselves if they were to get any help at all. Bill at least had something to tell the Minister of Health in Mongolia. "You can't set a clinic up for a bunch of nomads," he wrote in his very short report.

His last thought before he fell asleep on a yurt floor crammed with people, was a prayer to God that the Jeep would start in the morning. God in his mercy answered his prayer.

The trip into Mongolia put the country into the sights of the Baptist's International Mission Board. As a result, a doctor and permanent missionary were inserted.

Since the Mongolian people knew nothing about Christianity, there was no need for a church to go underground; there was no resistance to the gospel message at all. A missionary family, along with a doctor, was able to establish the first church there, and open the doors of Mongolia to the Christian message. The people were so eager to hear the story of Jesus and accept it, that the missionary pastor reached over three hundred people in his first year.

Once that happened, Bill addressed the next restricted country on his list.

Chapter 59
Strategy

The platform for entering restricted countries involved two main prongs. First, a strategy coordinator was assigned to the targeted area to figure out what needed to be done and design a plan to implement it. And second, the strategy coordinator had to establish a legitimate reason for people to come into that country. English teachers, businesses, and healthcare workers could go almost anywhere. They were all three in high demand by restricted countries, and as long as you didn't call them missionaries, they were fairly easy for the IMB to insert.

Almost all East Asian countries were eager to welcome American businessmen with the resulting opportunities for trade and the influx of American dollars. Getting in wasn't the hard part. Countries were anxious to get businessmen, health workers, and English teachers. Reaching people for Christ was the difficult part because it could get you arrested—or worse, killed.

Strategy coordinators were critical to implementing all of the work. They trained people for the intricacies of their mission, emphasizing the secrecy methods they would have to adopt. Explaining the methods they were going to use to secretly found underground churches, and how to gain the support of the people they met in their jobs.

Bill's job was to set up medical platforms. Health needs were rampant everywhere; every underprivileged country needed medical help, and it provided an open door for Bill to walk through, set up medical work, then bring in other doctors to staff the clinics.

Under the cover of medical assistance, he was able to set up strategy coordinators to expand missionary work in Laos, Cambodia, Vietnam, Malaysia, Thailand, and Tibet—along with Afghanistan, Kashmir, Pakistan, and other countries that wanted the American doctor to bring the free medical care he provided, and the teams of doctors and medical people he brought with him.

Every time he entered a country, he was able to visit underground churches and encourage them—since he had a legitimate reason to be there. He was a doctor; he had an excuse for contacting those missionaries who had been inserted while remaining under the radar—giving medical attention to the local people in the areas where churches had been established.

When a missionary or his family had a problem, Bill could easily cross borders, get in and clear it up—or get them out, without coming under suspicion himself. But he was always wondering if today was the day he would get caught.

Chapter 60
Tibet

Having opened the door to Mongolia, Tibet was a natural region for Bill to try and enter next. Both Mongolia and Tibet had been part of a swath of terrain under the control of Genghis Kahn stretching from Russia all the way to southern China. Both countries had been part of the Mongolian Empire—speaking the same language and having the same culture.

But when China took a huge chunk out of the center of the Empire, the two countries were severed, disconnected, and no longer part and parcel of each other. China carved out the middle ground between them and annexed it, separating Mongolia from Tibet by 7,252 miles—effectively destroying their communication with each other. Russia claimed Mongolia in the North, and China absorbed Tibet in the South, even though Tibet continued to consider itself an independent country.

It wasn't. Tibetans were now under Chinese control whether they liked it or not. Their benevolent rule by the Dalai Lama was constantly under siege by the Chinese Communists who demanded that Tibet acknowledge the fact that the Mongolian Empire was over and done with.

Bill stepped off the plane onto the top of the world in Tibet, 11,000 feet high. It was a country above every other nation on the earth—rising into the stratosphere. Separated by the Himalayas on the one side, and China on the other. A place where passengers were met at the airport with oxygen. It was almost impossible to get enough oxygen just by breathing—since any altitude over 5,000 feet could cause altitude sickness.

At 11,000 feet, many passengers were sick the moment they set foot on the ground—and the crew he had brought in with him was going to visit monasteries as high as 14,000 feet.

Bill knew to take Diamox and advised all of the doctors he had brought with him to take it as well. Each physician carried a black bag they had packed with medications and instruments they might need. But one of the doctors, a cardiologist, wouldn't follow Bill's suggestion to take the anti-altitude-sickness drug. After all, he was a doctor himself. After only a few minutes of climbing stairs, the rest of the group left him sitting down and wheezing as they continued on their trek upward to a monastery they had come to visit. Bill's suggestions weren't ever questioned again. By any of them.

When they reached the monastery, it was empty. The monks had been forced into their living quarters and were being severely beaten by the PSB for some religious infraction. The Chinese hated the Tibetans and found numerous ways to punish them for practicing their Buddhist religion. Bill warned the doctors that Christianity was not going to fare any better. "Keep moving," he said. "We can't get into an altercation with the PSB or we'll end up in jail. Some things we can help—but stopping the PSB from beating monks isn't one of them."

Bill had been able to avoid most encounters with the PSB—because the Baptist's strategy coordinator for the area was an electronic engineer who kept Bill up to date as to where the PSB was and what they were doing.

All American phone lines had been tapped by the Chinese, and every person who came into the country had their conversations recorded—but the engineer had found a telephone line in a secluded place where he could hide and tap the line into any government bureau he wanted to listen to. He would tap, listen, and then disconnect without being discovered because he wasn't using an American's phone line. He kept Bill informed of the Public Security Bureau's locations. As well as anything else the government was planning to do.

One of the surprising things about the Tibetan people was their height. Young men, the Kahm of Lhasa, were six feet tall and over. They made their living managing kiosks and were very colorful. Their boots had metal heel taps, and you could hear them tap dancing from a distance as they strutted in front of their stalls. They carried all of their wealth on their bodies, including silver engraved sheaths around their waists that held a knife.

Fascinated, Bill took a picture of one of the men with his Polaroid. The young Kham asked how much would Bill take for the picture, and Bill replied, "I'll trade you the picture for your belt and knife."

The Kham removed his belt and knife—and the trade was immediately finalized. Bill was shocked that the Kham made the trade, but in retrospect, no one Bill met had ever seen a picture, much less one of themselves.

The first thing on Bill's agenda was to observe and learn everything he could about Buddhism—the religion of Tibet. He needed to know what he was up against as he introduced Christianity to a people who had never heard about it. But the questions he asked people seemed to have no answers. "Where is your Buddha?" he asked.

"Oh, there are thousands of them," was the answer he usually got.

"Where do these thousands of Buddhas live?" he asked. None of the people he questioned had ever seen a Buddha, but they believed that the Buddhas were real and alive.

"Where are they? What do you do when one of them dies?"

The people didn't seem to know but would answer, "He's somewhere. He doesn't die, he reaches Nirvana or comes back as another Buddha."

Bill was learning one thing: Tibetan Buddhism was very different from Chinese Buddhism.

The second thing on his agenda was to set up a free medical clinic for the Tibetan people. He had brought a team of ophthalmologists in with him to do surgery on the blind to remove cataracts—giving them their sight; it was sure to draw a crowd. But for those who had other optic problems such as glaucoma, they could only dispense eyedrops; they were not a cure, but they had no other meds to give the people. Some things required care beyond the medical help they could share. But it was something, and people were pleased with anything they got from the American doctors.

It was so cold that they had to put a hot-pot beneath the surgical table to keep their feet from freezing. The number of cases they were seeing was so numerous that Bill put Janet to work as a nurse, handing lenses and surgical equipment to the doctors.

So many people needed cataract surgery that the ophthalmologists could only replace a lens in one eye per person. Bill and an older doctor—who could no longer do surgery—screened the people who wanted medical help, ruling out those who had retina damage or some other trauma that cataract surgery wouldn't help. The team didn't have enough lenses to do more.

After surgery, patients were overcome with emotion when they could see, when they were no longer blind. It gave Bill an opportunity to share the story about Jesus touching a blind man's eyes and allowing him to see clearly. "We have given you sight with your eyes, but Jesus will give you sight for your soul," he told the patients.

One of the American ophthalmologists wasn't able to adjust to the culture of the people he was dealing with. When the group shut down for the day, a Public Security Bureau member, who had been assigned by the Chinese to check up on them, asked if that doctor would examine his eyes. "No," the ophthalmologist said. "We're through here. We're done. You should have gotten in line with everyone else."

He then walked off and went back to his room.

Bill's impulsive lab tech Mike, stormed into the surgeon's room and yelled at him, "We don't want your help anymore—and if you leave this room, I'm going to beat you up. We aren't going to give you a chance to offend the PSB again. We need them on our side. You, on the other hand, are a royal jerk."

There were always interpersonal problems for Bill to deal with. Christians were, after all, human.

The Tibetan people readily accepted Jesus; they had no problem with multiple gods. They carved statues of Jesus and set them next to their images of Buddha. It looked like the idea of One God was going to take Bill a little while longer to explain.

Chapter 61
Tuberculosis

One of the more serious medical problems Bill planned to research in Tibet was tuberculosis. TB was a critical problem in all of the Asian countries, but there had not been any research done on how extremely high altitudes affected the medical culture tests for TB. Bill asked Mike, the lab tech who had threatened to beat up the ophthalmologist, "Would you go up with me to this Tibetan village and run some altitude TB tests for me? It's the highest berg I can find that we can get transportation to."

They boarded a round-trip bus which eventually dropped them off—high up in the stratosphere of Tibet. Neither of them had any idea where they were. They didn't speak the Tibetan language, and didn't know the bus schedule, but hoped the bus would loop back and pick them up on its next go around.

It seemed like as good a place as any to start doing the tests. They hiked in the direction of a small village, and on the outskirts, they came across a group of women thrashing barley, which was the only grain that would grow at that altitude. Near the women, a Tibetan man was slaughtering a yak. A huge man, covered in blood, wielding a machete and loading the severed limbs of the yak onto a wooden cart.

Fascinated, Bill began to take pictures. The Tibetan butcher looked up, saw the two white men with round eyes, picked up his blood-covered machete, and moved toward them. It was definitely not what they were expecting. They were justifiably terrified—they didn't know whether to run, hold their hands in the air, or fall to their knees.

The man reached out his blood-covered hand, took the Polaroid camera and the picture away from Bill, examined it, backed up, pushed a button, and snapped a picture of Bill and the tech. Grinning from ear to ear, he watched the picture roll out, handed the blood-smeared camera back, and held up the picture for the women to see. He grinned. Pleased with his trophy.

"This would be a good time to be able to speak their language," Mike whispered to Bill. His voice was shaking.

"I think it's a good time to take one more picture of this guy and then get out of here," Bill replied.

"We can't leave. We have to wait on the bus. Let's see if we can do some TB tests and take another picture. He didn't kill us, so what do we have to lose?"

When the bus returned, they had ten TB tests along with a Polaroid picture of a man holding a machete dripping with blood. All in all, a successful trip.

"You realize that we have to come back here in three days and do the final step on these TB tests?" the tech reminded Bill. "Or trash them?"

"You don't want to trash them after all we went through to get them! Do the preliminaries, and we'll think about what to do later. The guy with the machete liked us. We'll just need to get a better Polaroid camera and lots of film. This camera's finished. It's covered in yak blood."

"Got'cha. Will do."

Chapter 62
Becoming a Monk

The next day, Bill and Mike decided to scope out a local temple where monks supposedly knelt to chant, and were said to somehow vocalize three sounds all at one time. "Can't be done," an ENT specialist told Bill. "The vocal cords can't do that. You can make two sounds—sometimes. Three—not possible."

Mike was always up for an adventure, and Bill wanted to get to the top floor of the temple—which was forbidden. He wanted to be able to survey the surrounding area from above. Doing something illegal was nothing out of the ordinary for him, but after the incident with the machete, he wasn't feeling all that confident and pushed Mike up the stairs ahead of him. They climbed, fairly sure that the signs on the walls—which they couldn't read—said, "No entrance."

They could clearly hear the monks inside the temple—and as each individual chanted, they were able to verify that each monk could, indeed, make three sounds all at once.

In the streets below, people gathered in the courtyard to worship Buddha. Many had bloodied their knees from the act of contrition. They had crawled to get to the temple, some of them for more than a mile.

Mike poked around the roof landing area, found a closet full of robes, and gave in to temptation. He put a robe on, handed another to Bill, then leaned over the top of the parapet and stretched out his arms as if he was giving a blessing to the people who were in front of the temple. There was a roar from below as the worshippers on the ground began to raise their hands to heaven, then bow and offer oblation to the unknown priest wearing a religious robe on top of the roof. Bill should have known not to bring Mike with him to an off-limits place.

"Get that thing off before they storm us," Bill yelled.

They made a hasty retreat, slipping down the stairs while the chanting was still in progress. "I'm not taking you with me anywhere—ever again!" Bill told Mike. "You always find a way to get into trouble."

"You didn't have to put the robe on," Mike said.

"You didn't have to lean over the balcony and imitate a priest!" Bill replied.

That night, the duo attended a party with the rest of their team. To get there, they walked along the dark streets at the top of the highest country in the world. There were no street lights, and millions upon millions of stars covered the open sky, unlike anything they had ever seen. It was an awesome sight in contrast to the squalor of the day.

A group of Buddhist monks had been invited to dine with them—as guests of the medical group. When they started to eat, the monks sat silently with their hands folded in their laps. Bill looked at Mike—who was looking at him. "What?"

Their Tibetan interpreter intervened, "The monks were told to wait to start eating until after you prayed. They were told that Christians pray to their God before they eat their meal."

Chagrined, Bill and the rest of the party of Christians bowed their heads, "Lord please bless our food. And forgive us our indiscretion in the presence of these people who do not know you. Amen."

"Do you think this is roasted yak," Mike whispered to Bill.

"Just eat it. It's been blessed," Bill replied.

Chapter 63
Woman's Work

Janet was not a med tech or a doctor. She had adopted a different method of service. She was the strategy coordinator for an area that covered thousands and thousands of square miles in southern China.

To cover up what she was actually doing, she had set up a business there—finding and exporting native handicrafts while she secretly assisted in organizing churches. There were still some Chinese people remaining in the area who had survived the Christian purge that had been led by Mao and the Communists. As those Christians learned who she was, they began to surface to help her, risking their lives in the process.

Her position had not come easily—Baptists had deeply ingrained reservations about putting a woman in a position of authority over men. But the Asian IMB director had gone to bat for her and argued on her behalf. He strongly recommended her for the position and urged the IMB to give her the job, because she was by far the most qualified person. The IMB relented. She became a strategy coordinator but wasn't allowed to lead a church. She was, after all, a woman.

Missionaries in her area were able to get medical services quickly for their people—since Janet's husband was a doctor. He could be reached almost immediately in an emergency. She and Bill worked as a team—even though they worked in different cities in different capacities most of the time. Ships crossing in the night.

In addition to medical services for her area, getting Bibles into China was a priority. Printing them in Mandarin, then smuggling them into China for distribution was difficult. Those Christians who volunteered to carry them inland sometimes didn't make it back out.

They usually went in by train or plane, checking a bag full of Bibles and taking a roll-on for themselves. If the suitcase full of Bibles cleared entry, the carrier clipped the ID tag off so that there was no way to identify who it belonged to. Then picked it up on the other end when nobody claimed it. The danger of getting caught was always a possibility.

Bill had been working with an organization called Open Doors for a man who was commonly known as God's Smuggler—Brother Andrew. He had bought a van for Bill, which had simplified transport somewhat. After the Bibles were safely smuggled across the border, there was a covert arrangement for the carrier to sit down on a park bench with their suitcase full of Bibles and read a book. The pickup contact would sit down beside the smuggler, and also begin reading a book. They didn't look at each other or speak. After a bit, the carrier would get up and leave the suitcase on the bench. There was never any verbal contact for the transfer. The carrier and pickup contact were strangers and would never meet again. Safety was insured by the fact that they couldn't identify each other.

If a Westerner was caught smuggling, the Bibles were confiscated. If they were Chinese, they were arrested. Janet never knew what happened to the ones who didn't come back. Whether they were dead, alive, or locked up in jail. Whichever way, it wasn't good, and her operation was always on the edge of being discovered.

Their lives were hectic. Scheduling time for their family as best they could. Sending their two sons to Taiwan to an English-speaking Christian school. Flying them back and forth on holidays and summers. Knowing the dangers of air travel in that part of the world. It was the hardest part of being on the mission field—being separated so often from their boys.

Traveling by plane was a constant in all of their lives. Janet had flown on an assignment to south China in which an engine failed. The attendant assured her, "Don't worry, we have two engines. The other one is fine."

Later, when she took a group of doctors in, they connected at the airport and continued by car. Their driver pulled out into oncoming traffic and they had a terrible wreck. Everyone in the car was injured. Broken bones, broken teeth, and blood everywhere. Janet had four broken ribs. The injured doctors immediately began to use the equipment they had brought in their black bags to stop the bleeding and set fractures for each other since medical help in the area was nonexistent.

One of the doctors asked Janet, "Is it OK to take a picture of this to show my church when I go home?"

He didn't want to do anything illegal and get locked up, but pictures were a really big deal to the volunteers who went into China's interior. They wanted to authenticate their trip to their home churches. Including wrecks, blood, and broken bones.

Bill had recruited and inserted a medical team into Janet's territory to try and set up a clinic at the bottom of a steep mountainous Chinese range. People came from all over when they heard that medical care was going to be available. Bill brought a surgeon, a physician, and a dentist with him—along with as many medications as they could carry, but they quickly ran out of supplies.

By the time they got to a young boy who had malaria, they had nothing left to treat him with. All they could do was share the story of Jesus, explain that they were his helpers, and promise the boy that they would come back soon with the medication he needed. The entire purpose of bringing doctors in was to tell people about Christ as they ministered medical help.

The boy's family took him home to a tiny village in the uppermost mountains to wait. When Bill returned with the boy's medication, he gave it to one of the people on Janet's team to deliver. There were no roads to the top of the mountain, and by the time the team member got there, the boy had died.

The medical team was devastated, but the boy's family said, "Our son told us about your Jesus that likes to help people and take them to heaven when they die. We want to know him, too."

The boy's family and the rest of the village trusted in the doctor's Jesus. It was a sad and joyous event. A boy had died, but a village was saved.

Eventually, that kind of up-and-down emotion takes a toll on you if you don't find some sort of balance. Janet painted. It was an escape. Her work as an artist was included at a gallery in Macau, and the Chinese invited her to participate in their exhibition. The only white woman ever to receive that honor. The Chinese people loved what she did—they especially loved the fact that she wanted to learn and paint Chinese stylism, and that she did it very well.

Chapter 64
Where Am I

Cambodia, Laos, Vietnam, Indonesia—in country after country Bill set up medical services. The first time into a country he would usually come at the request of their health department—if they had one. Everyone wanted the American doctor to come and assist them because he brought them free modern health care.

The second time in, he would connect with businessmen, health workers, or teachers that the IMB had inserted to secretly start underground churches. By the third or fourth time he entered, he was uneasy—there was always the possibility that he would be caught. Eventually, there is a price to pay for living undercover and doing something that a country doesn't want you doing, but that was the price he paid to get in.

His reputation had been established. Word had spread quickly about the American doctor who would help a country with their medical problems and needs—a doctor who also brought teams of medical personnel with him as well as critically needed medical equipment.

His main work continued to be going underground into China, but requests for medical help were flowing in from other places in Southeast Asia.

He realized that he needed to expand his territory, but for every new place he went, there were diseases for which he had no resistance. He contracted typhus in Cambodia from sand fleas, Dengue fever in Malaysia. Coccidia—a stomach-bacteria in China. A fungus in Cambodia. Skin parasites—scabies—in Kashmir. Parasites were everywhere. He contracted giardiasis, a parasite that inflamed the stomach, more times than he could count.

Food sanitation was non-existent. Janet almost died from dysentery in Thailand. Mosquitos were rampant. Malaria and Dengue fever were common. He took eleven doctors with him to China where they were served fish that wasn't completely cooked. All twelve became deathly ill from an amoebic infection. The local medical personnel offered acupuncture—which all of them tried. Of course, it didn't help. There were no medicines to help them. Bill lost forty pounds in two weeks from the fish incident.

As if the diseases weren't enough of a hazard, he broke his foot in China, had a heat stroke on a mountain in Hong Kong, tore a muscle in his back in Bangkok, and had to crawl on his hands and knees to get back to his hostel. He had a spine abscess in China and tore an arm tendon in Macau. East Asia was full of opportunities for injuries and diseases that could kill you.

And if accidents or diseases didn't get you, there were always dangers in unstable countries like Cambodia. The UN had been called in as peacemakers—and thought their job there was finished; they were pulling out to the east. But the war was still raging between the Khmer Rouge and the Khmer Blanc in the west. The Cambodian strategy coordinator wanted to get in and establish a clinic there, so Bill flew from Phnom Penh into western Cambodia where the Khmer Rouge was still active—trying to determine what could be done medically to help the people who lived there.

While he was there, one of the warring combatants threw a hand grenade into a Bible meeting, blowing a child's legs off. The Communists controlled the area and didn't want Christians coming into their territory. Killing or maiming someone was the norm for the Communist Khmer Rouge. The UN may have decided that the war was over. The Khmer Rouge and Khmer Blanc, who were enemies, hadn't.

He eventually made it safely back to Phnom Penh. While he and one of the medics he had taken with him were eating in a sidewalk café, the medic began to chew on the ice in his drink. "Don't eat that ice!" Bill warned him.

He pointed to a truck which was unloading ice onto the sidewalk covered in spit, slime, and filth. "That's what's in your glass. Don't drink the water, or eat the ice. Don't drink anything unless you've watched it being boiled—or opened a sealed bottle you uncapped yourself. You should never drink the water or eat the ice in a third-world country."

In countries like Vietnam, Cambodia, Laos, and Malaysia, many times the only way he could reach the areas where he needed to go was to hike through jungle on foot. Wading through swamps of knee-high elephant grass looking for reclusive huts that sometimes rose over water on stilts—then hiking back out and spending hours picking leeches off of his legs.

Chapter 65
Other Dangers

A former Air Force intelligence officer, who was currently supervising some of the work Bill was doing treating malaria, went in with him to survey Laos. Southern Laos had only one questionable hospital—made of sticks, which was hard to even identify as a building; their medical practitioners were using methods from the dark ages. They were using salt water to treat malaria—which of course hadn't helped patients at all.

Back in Hong Kong, the two men had stuffed their suitcases with Laotian money to take in with them—money that would grease palms if necessary, and get them access. The money had been pouring in from Vietnam vets who wanted to help implement mission work to build clinics or hospitals.

There were differing opinions as to why so many vets were sending money. The Air Force intelligence officer who had come into Laos with Bill thought that perhaps it came from feelings of guilt for the war the American government had waged—and thought that some of the vets might have severe and lingering doubts about the part they had played in the war as well.

Bill had no interest in building hospitals; he had come to Laos under pressure from the strategy coordinator simply to see what could be done there. He wanted to establish clinics and underground churches.

"We need to get into East Laos, along the Vietnam border," Bill told his companion. "We can spend some of this money to improve the hospital here, but then let's move east. There's no medical service in the southeast at all. None. It would be a great opportunity for us to establish a clinic."

"No," the intelligence officer replied. "We can't go in there. Not east of here."

"Why do you say that? Why not?" Bill asked. "It's a wide-open opportunity."

"Land mines. Land mines are everywhere along the border."

"How do you know that?"

"I put them there. Dropped them during the Vietnam war. Air Force was tasked with dropping thousands and thousands of mines on the border—to keep our troops from being attacked from the west by the enemy. Trust me, you don't want to go in there. You won't be able to keep from tripping over a land-mine. They're everywhere. No way anybody could have cleaned up all that mess since the war ended. We're not going there."

Having given up the idea of a clinic in Eastern Laos, Bill moved on to a beautiful island off the southern coast of China—where he only lasted a week or two. Vietnam and China were still at war with each other, and while he was on the islands, the Viet-Cong began to shell it. Swamp, landmines, leaches, and jungles he could manage. Bombs were another thing altogether.

However, Vietnam wanted him to come in, bring ultrasound equipment and teach them how to use it, so he decided to try it. A few of the medical students he recruited to go in with him had made friends with the National Minister of Health in Da Nang, taught her how to play poker, and won her over to the idea of traveling with them to scope out the northern territory. As a result, Bill was able to move north through the country because his medical college recruits had found them an official government guide in a poker game.

When Bill flew into Bac Tai Nguen, fifty miles north of Hanoi, the stewardess on the plane confiscated each passenger's gun, made a hook from a coat hanger, looped the guns through their trigger guards and hung them up out of reach of the passengers. Almost everyone on the plane had a gun. It was an unnerving reminder that they were headed to a war zone.

When they arrived, the local magistrate told Bill that he looked like he was the right age to have been a soldier in the American military during the Vietnam war. He added that many of the patients he would be treating were local veterans of the war with America, and had been exposed to agent orange. Then asked, "Did you take part in the United States military assault on our country?"

It was one of those moments when you didn't want to tell the truth and get yourself killed. But he said a silent prayer and answered, "Yes. I was—

however, I didn't fight in the war; I was a flight surgeon in a training squadron in the states. Is that going to cause problems for me here?"

"No. No, it's OK," was the reply. "We threw out the French; we threw out the Chinese and after that, the Americans. You were just one more war for us."

Chapter 66
Islam

Eventually, the IMB asked him to evaluate Pakistan, and danger was raised to an entirely new level. The Muslim religion did not welcome Christians and actively killed infidels. And Muslims considered Christians to be infidels. Dangerous infidels. Bill now had an X on his forehead.

He had never considered crossing into Muslim countries. He couldn't speak their language and had minimal interest in trying to break through the Islamic religion. Everywhere he had been so far was Chinese or Mongolian. Buddhism, Taoism, and other strange religions came with an accompanying creed or idol. His expertise was in Chinese and oriental cultures so when the call came for help from the Strategy Coordinator of the IMB for him to go into Pakistan, which was a Muslim country, he was surprised.

"Why me," he asked.

"You're all we have," was the reply.

British Petroleum was testing for oil on the Pakistan border with Afghanistan, and had not had any luck in establishing hospitable relations with the Taliban. The IMB coordinator for Pakistan was good friends with British Petroleum's representative—who was also a Christian.

They had put their heads together and come up with an idea that might work: offer some kind of humanitarian program to Pakistani people that the government might embrace—and give it to them free of cost. British Petroleum would pay for it so that they might get their foot in the door to test for oil in the name of humanity. And Bill was a guy who knew how to get his foot through a door.

"Can you come give us some direction on how to go about establishing a healthcare facility here," the Pakistani coordinator asked Bill. "Act as an advisor and find out how we might go about offering some humanitarian aid that could give us a way to get into Pakistan. What we would need to do, or provide, and how we would need to go about it?"

"Sure," Bill replied. "I can do that, but I have to have a visa and a valid reason to be there. And government approval."

"I'll set it up, fly you into Karachi. Only problem you'll have will be that the flight arrives at 10 at night, and the flight out to Islamabad won't leave until five the next morning."

"No problem," Bill said. But in his own mind, he knew it would be a problem. He had never been inside a Muslim country. He didn't know the language and dreaded a seven-hour layover in a strange airport. However, the biggest problem would be that he had no knowledge of the culture and customs of Muslims. You could unknowingly make some gesture that was a life-threatening mistake without even knowing you had done it.

The flight itself was uneventful, but as he stepped into the Karachi terminal, armed soldiers with rifles were everywhere. He looked around for a place to sit and wait for the connecting flight the next morning, but was immediately encircled by military personnel who shuffled him along the aisles in the terminal and through a door to the outside, then locked the door behind him.

He was instantly surrounded by a crowd of people including a group of men poking and pulling on him, trying to get him to choose their taxi. Mosquitos swarmed him, and between the bugs, the crowd, the hacks, and the exhaustion of the trip, he gave up, laid down on the sidewalk on top of his two suitcases so someone wouldn't steal them, and waited for airport personnel to unlock the door the next morning at five.

He was scared. He had no means of communication, no water, no protection, and nobody knew where he was. Except for God himself.

When the doors were finally opened the next morning, he shared a breakfast bowl of curry with the crowd, everyone dipping their naan, their bread, into a common bowl. No spoons, no plates. The night had been one of the most horrendous, frightening, and miserable times he could remember ever spending—welcome to Pakistan.

He took the morning flight to Islamabad, then boarded a bus to Peshawar for the last leg of the trip. Even though he had permission from the government to be in the country, he was going into a territory where government people themselves refused to go. It was completely controlled by the Taliban. British Oil flew personnel into the well site at Savi Raga by helicopter to avoid being ambushed on Pakistani roads. Their drilling site was heavily barricaded with concertina wire and guarded by mercenaries. It was a no man's land.

The governor of the province, Sharif—who later would become the president of Pakistan, met him in his office in Peshawar, the city where years later, Americans would assassinate Osama Bin Laden.

Sharif told him, "You have my permission to go south of here—if you are crazy enough to do that. But I wouldn't do it."

Bill was on his own.

Sharif invited him to dinner with his family; however, it was the kind of an invitation for which Bill didn't know the correct response. Was he supposed to accept, or was it simply a cultural gesture that he should politely refuse? Not knowing the culture was hard.

Some things he had been warned about. He couldn't go outside on Fridays because that was the day the Imams whipped up their congregations to wipe out the infidels. And he was definitely identifiable as an infidel to the Pakistanis. The color of his skin, his clothes, his eyes. He stood out like a sore thumb.

Sharif gave him a cross-country military escort for protection as he headed south to the drill platform, then left him to fend for himself.

Inside the drilling compound, dozens of railroad cars had been turned into living facilities where he was assigned an empty box. He had arrived without any major incident.

Each day, from that point on, Bill went outside the concertina wire of the compound and held clinics—with no protection. Setting up a tent, he offered medical help to the Taliban and people in the surrounding areas, trying to make a connection to see if medical care would help with public relations.

Each day, he set his tent up in a different location on an endless stretch of dirt surrounded by barren rock mountains. Reaching those locations was so difficult to navigate that before he was finished with his work in the area, his crew had destroyed two Jeeps, and a camel had to be brought in several times to drag them out of ditches.

Children were fascinated with the ongoing spectacle and came out from hiding places in the cliffs and crags where families lived in caves—to watch, and beg for candy. Soldiers also emerged from behind the rocks carrying rifles. They were fighters, wanting to see who this man was and what he was doing there.

It was Ramadan. And even though Muslims couldn't eat or drink until the sun went down, once people in the area heard that medical help was available, they walked many miles without food or water to get there.

A female Pashtun doctor who had become a Christian while in Med school had volunteered to come with him and help treat the women since a male doctor couldn't touch or treat a female. It was taboo to even look at her. Another Pashtun who was also a Christian and had trained at the University of Chicago also came along and translated for Bill.

Bill never knew his real name. Everyone called him 'The Lion'. He dispensed vitamin pills, rewarding the people according to how many miles they had walked—ten miles, ten pills, and then he told them about Jesus. Pashtun people made up the tribe of the Taliban—the military force who controlled the border. Having the two Pashtun Christians to translate was invaluable to Bill.

Within a few days, men wearing turbans and carrying rifles had surrounded the area where Bill had pitched his tent, yelling at him, "Move that tent; you can't put a tent here. You have to get out. You have to leave. Leave. Now."

The Pashtun Lion began yelling back at them, "This is a holy man! Wherever the doctor's tent touches the ground is holy. You can't come near unless he says so or you will be cursed. If he says for you to come, then you can, but do not step inside the tent unless he tells you to come in."

Everyone began to back up and get in line, surprising both Bill, the woman doctor, and The Lion himself. There were so many people to treat that Bill felt like he was just grinding them out. The tech was following up, giving them pills in the name of Jesus, counting the pills out according to the miles the person had traveled.

One man, obviously the commander of a military group, emerged from the throng—along with others who were helping him carry a rope bed that had an old man lying on it. "This is my father." The interpreter translated. "Heal him." The words were given as a military command.

The commander's father was barely alive. He had severe pneumonia, a high fever, and his breathing sounded like an old Maytag washing machine. Ca-chug, ca-chug. He was dying.

"I can't heal him," Bill told the Lion. "All I have is penicillin. I can give him that, lay him over to the side of the tent, and try to treat as many other people as I can before he dies—then we'll find out what is going to happen to us. We need to pray. This is in the hands of God."

Bill gave the old man the medicine, gathered his group together, and prayed, "God, you are our hope. Please have mercy on this old man and on my team. And protect us from these soldiers."

By late afternoon, the old man stood up—healed as only the hand of God himself can heal. His son, the commander, was so excited that he declared himself to be Bill's personal protector, staying by Bill's side with his rifle pointed at the crowds of people, taking charge of security and getting the crowd into an orderly line; warning the people who started pushing to get near the tent—warning them not to step on the holy tent ground.

Bill stayed for days with no way to report the situation back to the strategy coordinator. But when he was able to give a report, he said, "You would have to get a physician team in here, a husband and wife who can both treat people. They would have to work in a tiny Muslim hospital located in the north. I don't see the situation here to be feasible. The doctors would be isolated with no support. As for me, I'm leaving Pakistan. I'm glad to be getting out alive. British Petroleum is also leaving. The well was dry."

"You promised me a month in Pakistan," the strategy coordinator said. "How about going south to the UN International border hospital in Quetta? See if we can get something started down there. The UN dumps a ton of money into that area, with no follow-up. They drill water wells for the people for free, then leave without teaching them how to maintain them."

"It's a rat's nest down there," Bill replied. "All the wounded come across the border from Afghanistan into Pakistan to get treated at the Quetta hospital, and that war isn't going to go away. Pashtuns are going to keep on fighting Afghans, or the Pashtuns will kill each other if they can't find a war with anyone else. But if that's what you want, I'll go—see what can be done in the area of health care."

"Maybe we could try and set up a system for pure water, or sewage management. Repair the wells the UN drilled—maybe a mobile clinic for vaccinations since the UN and Red Cross won't let us do Christian ministry in their hospital."

"OK, I'll case it out. Try and figure out what we might do."

He arrived in Quetta, toured the hospital, identified himself as a Christian doctor, and helped the staff with the injured when he was asked. Rifles were stacked up outside the doors; surrendering your weapon was an absolute rule for being treated. Wounded men who had been trying to kill each other the day before were lying in beds next to each other, a truce declared until they were released.

However, Russian AK47 rifles could be purchased in the town for ten dollars. Peace wouldn't last long after the casualties were released from the hospital. Killing seemed to be the norm.

One of the wounded in the ward, a sixteen-year-old Afghan girl, was lying on a stretcher near death from loss of blood. A mortar had torn a huge piece of her shoulder off.

"Why don't you give her a transfusion," Bill asked the attendant. "She's going to die without blood."

"We can't. Nobody in Quetta has A negative blood; we don't have anything to transfuse her with."

"I have A negative blood," Bill told him. "Take mine."

The attendant was visibly shocked by the offer, and paged a nurse who questioned Bill, "Why would you give your blood to this girl?"

"Because Christ Jesus gave his blood for me. He saved my life—so now, my blood can save this girl. I'm a Christian. We are called to help the wounded and the dying."

A crowd gathered to stare at the procedure as the nurse hooked Bill's arm up with a direct line to the wounded girl, and blood flowed from one life to save another.

The news about the American doctor who gave his blood to save a Pakistani spread, making his time in Quetta easy. He reported back to the strategy coordinator that mobile clinics were indeed feasible in the area. "It only cost me a couple of units of blood," he said.

"How about going to Kashmir before you return here," the strategy coordinator asked Bill. "They've asked for someone to come evaluate their situation and you sound like you might be willing to do whatever needs to be done. We want to try and figure out if there is a way that we can put someone in there permanently sometime in the future."

"I know nothing about Kashmir."

"That doesn't seem to be a problem for you."

"No more blood."

"Just your brain. See what you think."

Chapter 67
Kashmir

One more country to evaluate where he didn't know the language or culture. He took a plane back to Islamabad then boarded a grasshopper flight into the small province of Kashmir—flying between the mountain peaks of the Himalayas, which soared much higher than the small plane could reach to fly over them. India on the east, China on the north, and Pakistan on the west.

Getting to the people who needed help was almost impossible in the Himalayas. You had to cross makeshift bridges between the mountains. Heading in country, Bill crossed one bridge made entirely of rope swaying erratically over a deep gorge carved out by an untamed rushing river. Everyone endangered their lives trying to hold on, fight the wind, keep from falling off and plunging to their death—a frightening experience that most people wouldn't attempt unless they were on a mission from God.

Every person he saw had sores on their bodies where they had scratched themselves until they were bleeding—almost everyone was infected with scabies. Parasites under the skin. And lice. Two scourges, lice and scabies. Treating people was a dead-end endeavor. Even if you got rid of the parasites, the patient would immediately be re-exposed and reinfected.

He evaluated. Then sent in the identical report he had sent from Pakistan. You need a doctor. Preferably a couple. He didn't anticipate that there would be any response. But someone actually answered the request. Insane! It was another adventurer who later became Bill's best friend. He was endowed with the same ability to do what most people wouldn't even consider trying to do.

The missionary moved his family to Kashmir and stayed there until the Kashmir government discovered that he was a Christian and kicked him out—however, he didn't go back to America, he continued to work in Muslim countries for the rest of his ministry—until the diseases of the area destroyed his health.

Bill worked in and out of Indonesia, Malaysia, and Thailand, teaching for weeks on end, then getting back home to Hong Kong exhausted after every trip. Each trip was a validation for him that for certain, absolutely certain, he had not been called to go to Muslim countries. He was more than willing to turn it all over to his good friend in Kashmir. Glad to be back in Hong Kong.

Chapter 68
The Train

Thirty-seven years in China changes a man. But the one thing that never changed was Bill's drive to use his medical expertise to open up Christian work in closed countries. Even when his own health was shattered.

As he was stepping off the underground train in Hong Kong one morning, headed for the airport to meet a new young incoming missionary, he stepped down onto the platform, and the door of the train slammed shut on his left foot—trapping him.

The train began to move, dragging him with it down the platform toward a tunnel—where he could not avoid being crushed against the tunnel wall. He grabbed a pole on the landing and held on for his life, frantically yanking and jerking his foot loose from the door of the moving train. Pain infused his body as he finally tore free.

He fell onto the concrete platform still holding onto the pole, gasping for breath, his body infused with adrenaline flooding his sensory perceptions.

"I'm alive," he whispered. "Thank God." He let go of the pole, struggled to get up—and couldn't. When he tried to get to his feet, he realized that his left leg didn't work. He couldn't stand up. He had no feeling in his leg at all.

Years of medical training kicked into gear as he evaluated what was wrong. It wasn't good; he had seen this kind of injury before. Every tendon and ligament in his left leg was torn at the hip. Even the nerves to the muscles that joined the hip to the pelvis were no longer completely attached. Not only was he crippled, but he immediately knew that he was irreversibly crippled. He had saved his life, but this injury was permanent. He had probably lost the use of his leg. There was no way this injury could be fixed.

Disinterested crowds rushed around him, stepping over him as they pushed and shoved him to get on the next train. Finally, a toothless, grizzled old man who wasn't fast enough to elbow himself through the hoard of people and board the train, took mercy on him, stooped over, and helped Bill drag himself to the wall, where he propped himself up and waited for help.

Bill lay in a bed in the Hong Kong Baptist Hospital, attended by Chinese doctors. Doctors who whispered to each other about the injury—as if Bill didn't understand the extent of the injury himself. A number of those doctors had known him for thirty-seven years; one of them had delivered his youngest son, and knew the work Bill had done. Some of them were doctors who had gone into China with him, undercover, and were in awe of this medical pioneer of the East Asian continent. None of them wanted to be the one to tell him that he was permanently crippled.

He had considered retirement someday. Later. Not now. There was so much more work to do. But lying in a bed, being able to rest for the first time in years, having someone take care of him instead of the other way around, he admitted to himself that he was tired; the responsibility for evacuating people with critical health emergencies, diagnosing sickness or disease by phone or computer, and trying to ensure the safety of missionaries embedded in dangerous places, had begun to weigh heavy on him.

Getting them out when they had appendicitis, broken bones, complications with pneumonia, or a hundred other emergencies. Getting them out when they had been targeted, discovered to be missionaries instead of teachers, health workers, or businessmen. Before they ended up in jail or worse.

When he had started the underground work, there had been one or two who had come to help him, then a handful; now there were hundreds and hundreds of underground missionaries in almost every Asian country. Thirty-seven years had slipped by, hardly noticed. He was not a young man anymore.

He couldn't help but think back over incidents that made it all worthwhile. Working with a baby at Oceania in Virginia—a baby he had resuscitated two and three times a day, nurses yelling for him, telling him the baby was dying. Breathing life back into her—knowing it was hopeless, but doing it over and over again all day long.

He returned to that hospital's pediatric ward a year later and met a woman in the hallway holding a little girl's hand.

"Do you remember me?" she asked.

"I'm sorry, no. But your daughter, I think she may have been my patient," he replied.

"You saved her life," the mother said.

"No," he said. "God did that. All I did was to keep on trying and not giving up."

"The nurses told me you resuscitated her over and over again."

He remembered how exhausted he had been, and every time the nurses called him, how he kept asking himself why didn't he just let the baby go—she didn't have a chance in a million of making it. But here she was. Doing well. Holding her mother's hand. How many cases like that had there been in the last thirty-seven years since he had come to China? He fell asleep remembering all the people, all the people, all the people.

He was going to have to learn to walk with a leg that would never again cooperate. And a doctor with a gimpy leg wasn't going to be worth much in undercover work in East Asia. He had never thought about retiring; he had always pictured his future to be in East Asia. But obviously, things had changed. He was going to have to turn the work over to a new generation of James Bond mavericks with Bibles—undercover Christian agents.

He was going to have to leave East Asia, but he was leaving a system in place that would continue to spread the gospel all over China and surrounding countries.

He had built the work. He didn't want to turn it over to someone else—but it was inevitable; he was going to return to America, to a country that he felt like he no longer knew, to a country that didn't really know him anymore either.

Laying in the hospital bed, he realized that over the last thirty-seven years, he had become Chinese.

Chapter 69
Reflection

I walked up the stairs to the Oklahoma farmhouse with a wrap-around porch where my brother Bill was feeding hummingbirds. They flitted around darting back and forth, close to his outstretched hand, then joining dozens of others sipping nectar from a bird-feeder hanging from the eaves. He had a young chicken sitting on his shoulder; it cheeped occasionally and rubbed its head of soft feathers against Bill's ear.

"Where did the chicken come from," I asked him.

"An egg." He grinned, then added, "We got a few baby chickens from the local feed store, and this one followed me around from the day we brought them home. I got attached and couldn't condemn it to the chicken coop with the others. It likes me. Gives me someone to talk to. We both speak Chickenese."

He was so peaceful sitting there enjoying the birds that it was hard to imagine the chaos his life had been. His bum leg was propped up on the porch rail and a cane rested beside him on the swing.

"I hear you're still trying to save the world," I said. "News around town is that you're working with a mission organization here, with people who are destined for failure if someone doesn't rescue them. When are you going to take down your shingle? You're over seventy-five years old?"

"When I'm dead."

"That's what I figured."

He used the cane all of the time now; he had already endured four or five surgeries on his leg and back and actually looked good except that he had trouble walking. He dragged his left leg—but it hadn't stopped him, just slowed him down.

"Some of the locals told me that you and Janet started a church out in the low-rent government housing addition. Rented one of the rooms and started teaching. Also heard you started a Celebrate Recovery group for some of the folk in the area who are fighting addictions."

"Yep. Did that kind of rehab work over a hundred or so years ago in Virginia Beach. Only difference now is the new kinds of drugs. The problems people have don't change. Everybody still needs the right God in their lives."

I thought about my little brother and his dog Tango, running around the house, acting goofy, and having a wonderful time. And I thought about the man he had become and all of the things he had done. All of the doors he had opened in East Asia.

"They found a missionary's computer with the identity of all the other missionaries who were undercover there—and kicked all of them out of the country," he told me. "There are no missionaries that we know of in China anymore—of any denomination. The doors to China are completely closed now."

But I knew from what he had shared with me that behind the closed doors, there were still those Chinese people who had been reached, who had believed, and who still whispered in the dark, spreading the word, sharing the story of a man who died on a cross for our sin all the while praying that they wouldn't get caught. Chinese Christians who continued to spread the gospel within the Communist system, hiding from the Public Security Bureau as they told others about the good news.

My brother gave up his life to go to China. He helped heal their diseases and told them about Jesus.

God started a movement with one man, and thousands of others joined and followed God's call—continuing the work.

And many continue to die doing just that.

Epilogue

The events in this memoir of my brother are true. However, some of the dialogue and sequencing have been altered to abbreviate the story into a manageable account and make it more readable. I wish I could have included it all, but it would have taken thirty-seven years.

Printed in the USA
CPSIA information can be obtained
at www.ICGtesting.com
CBHW051045111223
2533CB00021B/130